I0039766

BALANCE

&

RE-BALANCE

LOST & HOW TO FIND IT

Written By
Jason B. A. Manny

Published By
Forays-Media

www.forays-media.com

first edition

2009

Published by Forays-Media

Copyright © Forays-Media
all rights reserved

ISBN 978-0-9563815-1-4

About the Author:

Jason B. A. Manny. Born in the early 1960 ' s,
with post graduate qualifications in
management and engineering. An independent
thinker with a longstanding interest in human
psychology as well as science and
mathematics.
This is his first published work.

PREFACE

In a world where
conflict is rife,
greed is prized,
crime is wild,
justice is scarce,
stress and depression are a norm,
a planet is scared,
and humanity is a struggle,

What is the unifying essence that has gone wrong?
and
Are we so far gone that we cannot put the world to
right again?

Who has the power for change?
and
Can it be done?

Most things involve a state of balance, without it, the
likelihood for chaos, destruction and disaster is
heightened.

But, to achieve a balance requires determined,
deliberate and focused actions that most often take
time.

That is at odds with the world of fast moving events
and the disposable societies of the early 21st Century.

i

CONTENTS

DIVINE AUTHORITY

Many people feel a need to search for and believe in a Divine Authority.

This is evident throughout human history.

A need to explain the mysterious powers of nature, from the pagan gods of the sun, moon, statues and animals, to the mythical Greek and Roman gods to the present day religions.

These religions provide a focal point for hope, prayers, fears and moral choices.

A belief in a religion offers a structured approach to a person's behaviour that is engendered by promised or anticipated rewards and by instilling a fear of sever consequences if the expected behaviours are not adhered to.

Most religions offer a set of rewards and punishments to their followers when they exhibit behaviours that are then judged by that religion.

Behaviours not permitted by a religion or are disapproved of, are discouraged with promises of divine punishments, whereas behaviours to be encouraged are associated with worldly and divine rewards.

A disbelief in a particular religion automatically forfeits any rights to any promised worldly or divine rewards that are offered by that religion. This acts as an encouragement for new recruits into that religion.

But why do we need any religion?

A simplified answer is that unrestrained behaviour can eventually lead to savagery.

Relying on governmental laws as a substitute for religion to guide human behaviour may not be as effective.

Few individuals nowadays are in awe of government!! The feeling that if a person can break a government law and get away with it, if they are not caught, does not offer the restraint to behaviour that is engendered by a belief in a divine power that is difficult to hide from.

RISK BEHAVIOUR

Human individuals do not all exhibit a consistent level of restraint over their behaviours even when faced with the same controls, promises and threats.

The range of characteristics exhibited by individuals is wide and varied and so is their risk behaviour.

The inclination to take risk is driven by self-interest and the desire to achieve a particular gain. But the readiness of an individual to take risk is likely to be moderated by two main individual characteristics:
the fear of consequences if the risk decision goes wrong, and
the self-conscious, self-implemented restraint that is the consequence of beliefs and the individual's own moral code.

It is often quoted that "High Risk can bring High Return" while "Low Risk is likely to bring a Low Return". This is almost an advertisement to encourage high-risk behaviour. What this statement does not allude to, is that risk may be high for two reasons that combine together
1) the low probability of success, and
2) the seriousness of the damage that the behaviour may cause

A High Risk-High Return behaviour may on very few occasions be very rewarding but is often damaging.

It is also often easier to destroy than it is to build up and create.

For a high-risk behaviour, the aggregate of a low count of success (low probability) combined with the seriousness of the damage (quality) from the large number (high probability of failure) of all the associated failures, will significantly outweigh the high return of the very few successes.

Averaged over a large number of attempts, the reward from a High risk-High return behaviour is very likely to be negative and is often destructive. Gambling is a case in point. The reason for the world wide credit crunch of 2007/2008 and the consequent damage to economies and societies is another case in point.

How much influence, fear has over risk behaviour compared to self-restraint will vary from one individual to another and most likely, from one time to another.

Fear as a moderator of risk behaviour could be considered as pure and natural risk aversion.

However, the self-restraint element could be considered as the self-control that is exercised in not pursuing our risk desires.

Unrestrained High-Risk behaviour is likely to be very damaging to the individual and to society. It should be avoided and restricted with a promise of severe penalties for those who exercise it.

On the other end of the scale, naturally risk-averse individuals will mostly exhibit Low-risk behaviour. This is a naturally safe behaviour but can stifle enthusiasm for change and growth. Although it is not a dangerous behaviour, it is also not a favourable behaviour.

The detailed interpretations of a particular situation will inform and influence judgements and may lead to minor variations in conclusions. However, the most beneficial behaviour is likely to be "Moderate" risk guided by self-restraint.

It is possible to simply categorise an individual's self-regulating ability into one of three groups:
    1- Fully self-regulating
    2- Moderately self-regulating
    3- Difficult to self-regulate

Some individuals may wish to place themselves in the "Difficult to self-regulate" category because it eases their conscience when they fail to self-regulate due to their lack of effort, even though they are not lacking in ability to "self-regulate".

However, most individuals may be categorised as 'Moderately self-regulating'.

The few 'Fully self-regulating' individuals can maintain a steady response to events and exercise self-control in line with their moral judgements and with little regard to other external influences.

Moderately self-regulating individuals exercise varying degrees of self-control that are influenced by their own self-interests such as greed, envy and power, and their own circumstances where external factors, including, group behaviour, peer pressure and tribal loyalties, are influential.

For those who require encouragement and greater determination to maintain appropriate self-regulation, they find it more difficult to be guided by governments and by the rule of law. Their self-restraint is diminished and their defiance is raised.

When presented with opportunities that appeal to their self-interest and do not promote the wider interests of the community or worse still, are in direct conflict with the interests of others, those individuals who need that extra leverage to exercise self-restraint are likely to find it increasingly difficult to rely on governments regulation and on law enforcement.

From the opportunistic thief to the premeditated murderer, with varying causalities and destructive consequences, the range of felonies from misdemeanours to serious crimes can be largely attributed to a lack of self-restraint.

This lack of self-restraint is probably also associated at times with inappropriate moral judgements, a devaluation in the interests of others and a disrespect for the harmony in society.

But, what about self-defence? we may ask.....
In the majority of situations where self-defence may be needed, if the aggression that at first initiated the situation was itself restrained, there would be no situation that requires self-defence.

However, where aggression has to be faced, offensive self-defence may still be questionable. It is often said that attack is the best form of defence, but two wrongs cannot make a right, especially if other options are available in protective self-defence and the avenues for conflict resolution are still available and possible.

To engender and enhance an individual's ability towards self-restraint, the character of the individual is a major consideration.

However, individuals are aggregates of nature and nurture. For some, nature is dominant. For others, nurture is more impacting. Therefore, there cannot be one approach to encourage self-restraint.

The only consistent fact for all individuals of all characters is that self-restraint comes from within, it cannot be imposed by law enforcement, even though law enforcement has a role to play in influencing an individual's psychology.

In fact law enforcement can at times have an opposite effect, contrary to expectations. This can and does happen when an individual has developed a particular belief that confrontation and rebellion are labels to be prized and to be sought after!

A lack of the fear of expected consequences alongside a lack of respect for governmental authority and for law enforcement organisations dilutes an individual's desire for self-restraint.

A world of instant access to information has brought people much closer to their human rulers, exposing the frailties and fallibilities of those rulers, governments and law enforcers to the masses that they are supposed to rule and govern.

BALANCE

Interacting with the world, nature, other creatures and other people, inevitably demands from an individual to constantly make moral judgements about themselves and about the world or the other people that they interact with.

On one level, this moral judgement is guided by the point of balance that the individual has grown to consider as acceptable.

When many talk about a "sense of right and wrong", they are generally referring to that point of balance relevant to a particular situation that they consider acceptable.

But who sets this acceptable point of balance?

In certain sets of unambiguous circumstances, the majority of people will instinctively and easily recognise similar points of balance despite the varying moral backgrounds of those individuals and their own evolved sense for the point of balance.

A universally recognised typical example that stems from an innate sense of self-preservation is that, premeditated and unprovoked murder is "wrong". Although, some may attempt to cloud that recognition by justifying certain acts falsely as self-defence!

Extreme situations often stand out and are generally more readily distinguished and categorised as "right" or "wrong" by the majority of individuals even when they disagree on their conclusions because their perspectives are at odds with each other. Take the common phrase

"One man's terrorist is another man's freedom fighter". This is an example of an extreme act that is judged differently from two opposing perspectives.

The reason for such wildly different judgements over the same extreme situation is that, individuals tend to judge an act as an aggregate of all its inputs and outputs and not in isolation. To reach similar conclusions, we need to have access to all the same inputs and to weigh them equally. For two different individuals from two opposing perspectives with their own self-interests at play, that is unlikely unless they exercise strict self-restraint.

It may be considered difficult for the ebb and flow of human society to operate within a state of balance with the world around it. But that balance is vital for the future survival of human society, within itself and within the world it occupies.

In older times, when geographical distances meant restricted communications that kept the then spread of humanity in isolated pockets around the world, these pockets of humanity developed separate societies and engendered their own separate systems of commonly recognised "rights" and "wrongs".

For each of those isolated communities, their own moral choices maintained a balance that suited their local physical environments and their local human self-interests. When the choice of balance was correct, most of those isolated pockets of human societies thrived and were self-sustaining. But when the choice of balance was wrong, many of those societies became self-destructive and eventually disappeared.

RELIGIONS AND RELIGEOUS EXTREMISM

Historically, religion has played a significant role in achieving a sense of balance and in helping to guide individuals towards common interests. Using prescribed behaviours attributed to divine authority.

Balances as prescribed by religion typically provide common starting targets for their human societies but automatically remove the individual responsibility in setting these targets. In doing so, the religion absorbs potential conflict of judgement between individuals over these issues. A role best performed by a higher power or so believed to be a higher power!

In the case of the Christian Church, it fulfilled that role well so long as individuals believed the church was a conduit for a higher power that had the right and duty to make such decisions.

From individual rulers and leaders to groups, bands and even whole nations, many have attempted, throughout history and right through to the present day, to justify or attach a sense of authority and credence to their judgements and actions by claiming some form of divine favour or an authority bestowed upon them by a divine power.

This claim of divine favour or authority is in the interest of making their judgements and actions more palatable to others. It is their attempt at appearing unquestionable and righteous so that their motives and actions are accepted without descent.

With a changing world, where the means of communications amongst populations is easy and instant, church and other religious organisations are more easily recognised as select individuals making choices on behalf of the masses.

As a consequence, it is becoming more difficult for Christian churches and other religious organisations to prescribe behaviours and points of balance when the divine attributes of those decisions are becoming more easily questioned and the human fallibility of religious leaders and religious organisations is becoming more easily recognised.

These factors are influential contributors for the movements towards fundamentalism in their attempts to access sources and scriptures that those individuals still believe to be directly received from higher divine powers that have reliably and authoritatively set the prescribed points of balance that those individuals need to believe in.

A STABLE SYSTEM OF BALANCE

In general, a system that has only one single point of balance, is a precariously balanced system that is easily destabilised. Like the ball that is balanced at the top of a pinhead.

For a system to be more stable, it must have a region of balance that allows it to flex and adapt to prevailing circumstances that are imposed on it while remaining within the bounds of its region of balance.

It may be suggested that the wider the region of balance, the more stable the system is likely to be. However, for a complex system, the wider the region of balance, the more elements will automatically exist within this region of balance that all have to be weighed against each other and balanced against each other to maintain the overall balance of the system.

A system with a single point of balance is more easily judged but is unable to accommodate multiple inputs. It is a simple, one-dimensional system as well as being easily destabilised.

At the other extreme, a complex system with a very wide region of balance and numerous input elements may be very difficult to manage. Consequently, such a system may drift out of balance because of these complex interactions within it and the difficulty in managing them.

So, how can we achieve an appropriate region of balance and establish what elements it may contain?

Many would make that judgement based on their own self-interest and are therefore likely to make choices that may appear correct for them but may be "wrong" from a wider perspective.

A better approach is likely to be that which includes all the necessary core elements for self-regulation and self-restraint, but then leaves a minimum set of checks and balances that are required to maintain an operational balance. We could refer to this as an "Optimal System".

Such an optimal system with a minimum requirement for checks and balances is likely to be a more efficient system that can be maintained with much reduced energy expenditure, leaving more energy available for our genuinely productive output.

The difference between an optimal system and a system that is not could be demonstrated by describing two hypothetical versions of the same situation.

The hypothetical versions used for the purposes of this example are for traffic flow through a residential suburban driving zone where vehicle speed is an important element in maintaining traffic and pedestrian safety:

Hypothetical version 1 (a typical traffic flow, a speed control-penalty system):
A system where the maximum speed limit is set at 30mph. Speed cameras, speed limiters and extensive law enforcement are used to prevent any driver from exceeding the set limit. If this limit is exceeded, the point of balance is considered to have been upset and the sustainability of the system stability is considered to

have been jeopardised. Much energy is invested into ensuring that the set speed limit is not exceeded and also into law enforcement should the set speed limit be exceeded.

Such a system could be categorised as oppressive. It engenders a negative reaction in most people and worse still, it would not prevent a careless or determined driver from causing the damage and injury to others or to property that it proposes to prevent.

Hypothetical version 2 (a possible optimal system):
A system that places great personal responsibility on a vehicle driver to be extremely mindful while driving not to cause damage or injury to others or to property. The driver is provided with a clear unambiguous guide of the preferred speed range for the traffic zone. A suggested speed range up to 30mph under average traffic environment conditions. Then the decision is left to the vehicle driver to choose the appropriate driving speed for the prevailing traffic conditions. Such a system would monitor traffic flow outcome that would only require intervention if and when a driver causes damage or injury to others or to property.

For this hypothetical version 2 example above, it is not immediately obvious why or how such a system could possibly function safely and sustainably.

The premise here is that, vehicle drivers who have a vested interest and do not wish to cause damage or injury will be guided by appropriate training and information provided to them before they are allowed to drive. This training should be good enough to allow a driver to make reasonable assessments of prevailing traffic, driving and vehicle conditions and of appropriate speed ranges to operate within.

Alongside this preparation for safe driving should be a clear understanding of their duty for self-regulation and self-restraint and the certainty of severe law enforcement consequences of not doing so. The severity of the law enforcement consequences must be pre-set at different levels, but these must all be absolutely clear to everyone, must be unwavering and must be appropriate to level of damage or injury caused.

By placing the power and decision for safe driving totally upon the shoulders of the driver who ultimately has the controls of the vehicle, this system is immensely simplified, and the individual is empowered to consider the interests and the welfare of the world around them. But equally, with authority comes responsibility. The individual must then be fully accountable for their actions.

The first Hypothetical version, with the speed control-penalty system, would not prevent undesirable damage or injury caused by bad or careless driving any more than the second Hypothetical version.

However, the second Hypothetical version, with its possible "Optimal System", would only be effective and work as anticipated if the need and ability for self-regulation and self-restraint are addressed and disseminated to become internalised by all road users and the consequences of failure are made clear and are strictly implemented, much as campaigns against "drink driving" have achieved in the UK.

SYSTEMS

What do we mean by a system, and how is that relevant to our view of balance and the world we live in.

To appreciate that, we need to clarify the interpretation we are using of what a system is and the how we can view the world we live in as a complex structure of interacting systems.

To begin, there are several dictionary definitions for a system. That most relevant to the context of this book is:

"a group or combination of interrelated, interdependent, or interacting elements forming a collective integrated and self-contained entity"

A system is characterised by the use of order, planning, classifying and categorising.

Therefore, a system requires the expenditure of energy and resources to maintain its steady correct operation.

Such an expenditure is a cost that has a psychological, physical or monetary form.

The entropy of a system, is a term used to represent the degree of disorder or lack of organisation within the system. It indicates the tendency for that system towards chaos and eventual disintegration.

Without proper controls, all systems tend towards chaos.

Efficient controls are able to maintain system stability at minimum cost and with least energy expenditure.

Man-made systems are often designed with modifying inputs that can be used to directly manipulate the points of balance within the system.

However, many naturally occurring systems have evolved with their own internally dynamic mechanisms that automatically interact to attempt to maintain the system within a particular region of balance under most naturally occurring external conditions.

For naturally evolved dynamic systems, it can be observed that, when one input element changes towards a boundary of the region of balance expected for it, then other input elements react naturally and automatically to change in an opposing direction to bring the balance back towards the central part of the expected region of balance for the system.

On occasions when external factors conspire to change particular input elements significantly and very quickly beyond their expected regions of balance, a naturally self-adjusting dynamic system may not be able to react appropriately or quickly enough to bring the system back to its region of balance. Such events are likely to cause a "Catastrophic" failure of a dynamic, naturally occurring system.

If human society is appropriately viewed as a system, then there must exist some proper controls, some naturally dynamic and some manipulated, to ensure its maintenance and stable operation.

In fact, it is possible to consider the whole universe as a single system, but it is also possible to consider parts of the universe as systems in their own right within the universe.

Such partial systems would interact together to make up the total system that is the whole universe.

Therefore, with a careful choice of appropriate boundaries, we can identify systems as well as systems within systems.

Within each system, changeable elements interact together to create the signature characteristics of that system.

In addition to the changeable interacting elements within the system, a system receives external input elements from surrounding systems and exerts external output elements on other systems.

One possible systemic structural view of the physical universe that we perceive, is to start with the whole universe as an encompassing system, then the Galaxies as systems within (for us, it is the Milky Way), then the Star systems within (for us, it is the Solar System), then the Planet Earth and its Moon System, then the Earth Envelope system (bounded by the Earth's atmosphere).

GLOBAL WARMING AND EARTH'S ECOLOGY

Within the Earth Envelope system, there are multitudes of other interacting systems that all have direct impacts on humanity. Most of these systems are natural parts of the earth envelope, others are man-made.

It is almost impossible to determine the extent of our human impact on the Earth's ecology compared to the impact of naturally occurring events.

However, there is no doubt that we have some direct influence on the Earth's environment that in return has a direct influence on us, as we all know.

That is why major issues that act as significant modifying inputs to the Earth's existing systems are of such importance. These include:
- the destruction of the rain forests and their associated systems
- the pollution of water resources and the atmosphere
- the burning of fossil fuels
- the use of nuclear energy
- the irresponsible exhaustive consumption of the Earth's bounties
- the destruction of whole species
- the introduction of genetically modified creations
- the building and use of weapons of mass destruction
…. a few amongst many others ….

Such elemental factors that are determined by humanity's own actions, interact directly with other earth systems to achieve a constantly changing state of balance within the Earth's envelope.

Any such state of balance is characterised by the measurable and the observable features we experience directly on earth. These include the weather, the oceans' currents, the sea level, the global temperature, the crops harvests …. and so on.

It would be difficult to underestimate the complexity of interactions within all these systems and sub-systems that influence the environment that we inhabit.

For example, there is no doubt that the observable phenomenon of "Global Warming" is genuinely taking place. However, it is equally true that we cannot be wholly certain about the mechanisms that exist and the degrees of influence they have over this observable output, the global temperature.

The observable changes in global temperatures are the result of effective readjustments of balances that are subject to the variety of inputs.

Many scientists are attempting to model the factors that they can, to predict the likely effect on our habitable environment.

It is also true that to model a system, we need to be as certain as possible about all the mechanisms employed within that system and how they interact with each other to produce a particular state of balance.

Yet another factor to consider is that a state of balance is often not achieved instantly, and that for a single change of a single elemental input, there could be a time lag before the system re-adjusts to a new state of balance.

Also, complicating the modelling process is the multitude of inputs and the changeable nature of many of those inputs. Each of those inputs may not be changing once but is changing constantly. They are dynamic inputs.

To make predictive models of a system, scientists frequently have to make judgements about what elemental inputs to include in the model.

Such choices of what elemental inputs to use in the models are often determined by:
- the degree of knowledge we have acquired about these elemental inputs
- the mechanisms they employ to interact with other inputs
- our knowledge and ability to define those mechanisms in a manner that can be modelled
- the degree of influence we believe that they have on the aggregate output, and
- the availability of historical data to test and verify the model's predictive power.

Scientists will often ignore or simplify certain parameters in the interest of being able to create a manageable model.

Even if our knowledge and our technology will allow us to identify and measure all the significant elemental inputs, and even if we believe we can understand and we can evaluate the mechanisms that these elemental inputs use to interact together, it is unlikely that we have reached that stage yet to model "Global Warming", and are unlikely to do so for a long time, if at all.

Also, our technology has existed for such a short period of time compared with the time scales employed by those elemental input interactions that affect the Earth's environment.

This means that we only have a brief snapshot of a Micro-sized view of a few of the elemental interactions and the prevailing changeable outputs that have recently existed on this earth.

It is necessary to recall that the Earth's environment is determined on a Macro-sized view over a significant length of time, with many time lags between inputs and outputs.

So, how can we be comfortably certain about modelling such systems when we are unable to verify these models even if they were comprehensively and correctly designed, which on this occasion is also unlikely.

Just to demonstrate an example of this explanation: It is likely that most models for predicting "Global Warming" would start by considering the earth as an object receiving heat energy from the Sun (heat gain) and radiating heat energy to the surrounding space (heat loss).

When the heat gained is matched by the heat loss, the temperature should remain constant.

However, there are many natural complicating factors. One of those is that some heat gain may be converted into energy stores within the earth systems and does not always result in increased temperatures.

Global Warming occurs when there is a net heat gain that contributes to a temperature rise. So how does that happen?

Not all of the Sun's energy reaching the earth actually enters the earth's atmosphere to heat the earth. Much of the Sun's energy is reflected back towards space in the upper atmosphere surrounding the earth, acting like a mirror, and can be considered part of the heat loss to space.

However, when the Ozone Layer in the upper atmosphere is damaged, a passage forms for more of the Sun's energy and damaging radiation to reach the earth.

Also, the gases in the Earth's upper atmosphere act as a mirror reflecting some of the Earth's radiated heat energy back to the earth, reducing the heat loss to space. These gases are what is commonly referred to as Greenhouse gases. Their presence results in less heat loss to space and a net heat gain to the earth.

One of the main Greenhouse gases in the atmosphere is Carbon Dioxide, which is naturally occurring but has been increasing in concentration as a by-product of burning more fossil fuels since the start of the Industrial Revolution. This is often used as a primary explanation of Global Warming.

Let us consider several issues that shed some doubt over the viability of such simple models:

First; The amount of energy emanating from the Sun towards the Earth is not fixed. It has been observed that the Sun 's heat output is variable and our predictions of those variations are limited to our recent observations.

Second; The Earth's orbit and its orientation to the Sun, change in a manner that would affect any net heat gain from the Sun. This is likely to be difficult to model and project forward over a long period of time.

Third; the heating of the Earth's crust and the Earth's Atmosphere is also due to heat radiating from the Earth's own molten core. This takes the two primary forms of:
- steady heat radiation by conduction and
- sporadic heat radiation by expulsion of molten lava directly into the atmosphere and into the oceans during volcanic eruptions

Fourth; Nature's own produced atmospheric pollution from sporadic and unpredictable natural events that are uninfluenced by humanity, such as volcanic eruptions and smoke from wild fires …etc.

These natural pollutants will influence the amount of heat absorbed from the Sun as it reaches the atmosphere, and are likely to be complicated to model and project forward over a long period of time.

Fifth; The actual process of "Global Warming" as it occurs, is likely to create changes within the Earth's envelope system, due to the changing atmospheric temperatures. The influences of these changes are very complicated to predict and model.

Some changes may enhance Global Warming, others may slow it down. All this is complicated further by the time lags and any subsequent knock-on secondary changes that are largely unknown.

Just to take a possible but uncertain scenario.
It is suggested that Global Warming is likely to change
the flow of the ocean's currents and subsequently change
the atmospheric weather patterns.

Over a period of time, that may change the various
prevailing temperature gradient patterns in the Earth's
own crust including, along the fault lines between the
various tectonic plates. That itself may cause changes in
the natural releases of the Earth's own heat from events
such as volcanic eruptions. These are likely to be
unpredictable and it would be very doubtful that they
could be included in a predictive model for Global
Warming.

Sixth; A rising Global Temperature may accelerate the
growth of vegetation, algae and plankton that will absorb
some of the additional energy and the Greenhouse Gases
that may be causing the Global Warming. The
consequent primary and secondary effects on life on
earth are complex and are not easily or reliably modelled.

Seventh; Rising Global Temperatures may alter the
natural and normally slow chemical reactions that take
place in nature like the various oxidisations that are
influenced by temperature.

Some of these reactions will absorb heat and lower the
temperature but consequently alter chemical balances
across the oceans.
The nature and extent of these primary and secondary
effects on Global Warming and on life on earth are also
very complex and are almost impossible to predict.

Eighth; In addition to the heat energy sources we considered so far to contribute to the balance of Global Warming, The Sun as a heat source and the Earth core as a radiating heat store, there are other sources that we may consider for the scenario:

- We burn fuels to generate heat and power. The world of the 21st Century needs electricity.
These fuels are the Earth's own natural stores of heat energy that are portions of heat energy received from the Sun over preceding millennia.
By burning these fuels for heat, electricity and power generation, we are releasing this store of energy and altering the balance that has been in the making for millennia.

- Also, we are increasingly releasing elemental energy on this planet that was never intended to be part of nature's set of balances within the Earth's Envelope system.
Nuclear energy is stored inside the fabric of matter. It is the energy of creation that binds together the matter that makes up our physical world.

The Sun's own heat energy is the result of releasing nuclear energy from the Sun's own gases.

The release of nuclear energy within the Earth's envelope by nuclear weapons and weapons testing, and in nuclear power generation plants is like introducing a very small piece of the Sun directly into the Earth's ecological systems.

This may also be a direct contributor to Global Warming. Its significance will depend on the extent of nuclear energy generated and released.

The above were just a few but not exhaustive examples of the reasons why predictive models for "Global Warming" are likely to be limited and unreliable.

This is not intended to dismiss the genuine "Global Warming" phenomenon, but only to demonstrate the principle that this Earth is a complex system of balances that are constantly changing and naturally re-adjusting.

Global Warming may or may not be primarily due to man-made factors. None-the-less, this Earth may be able to re-adjust to the various input changes, or may reach a new point of balance that may or may not be a point of balance suited to our habitation.

So long as our needs and our industry in our human societies drive us towards releasing the buffer of stored energy on the face of this earth, humanity will continue to be a net contributor of heat towards Global Warming, however insignificant.

It should be our duty as it is in our own interests to minimise our impact on the Earth's ecology.

Any major and relatively sudden changes to the Earth's ecology will inevitably act as significant influences towards imbalance. This would result in the Earth's systems attempting to re-adjust themselves to reach an appropriate region of balance.

But the greater the imbalance, the greater is the turmoil created and the longer are the time scales needed for a re-balance to be achieved. In the mean time our habitable environments are seriously disrupted while this re-balancing process takes place.

To reduce our potentially undesirable impact on the Earth's ecology, a starting point would be to consider the objective of an efficient energy-neutral habitation as desirable even if it is not practically achievable.

The path leading towards becoming heat energy-neutral while, at the same time fulfilling our needs and the requirements of our industry, is the process of harnessing and using renewable energy from solar, wind and hydro alongside a much diminished use of fossil fuels and nuclear energy.

Not forgetting that no matter how environmentally friendly and ecologically sensitive we may become, human society, by the nature of its existence and its survival needs alone, will continue to alter the Earth's environment and will continue to impact on the Earth's resources.

The Earth's natural ecology is a multitude of systems that are constantly changing and re-balancing, with a natural process of change that results in naturally changing habitations, weather systems, species mixes …etc.

While these changes take place in small steps over a relatively long time, their impact on total balances will hardly be observable over a short time scale. But over a long time scale, we can observe many historical natural changes such as:
- the Earth's temperature fluctuations resulting in the historic "Ice Age"
- the extinction of species such as the Dinosaurs and the mammoth
- the emergence of new species through evolution and natural selection

- the changing sea levels resulting in inland sea beds evident by sediment samples from all over the world … etc

The important point to recognise is that Earth's ecology is naturally changing but slowly. Therefore, any attempts on our behalf to try and preserve the Earth's ecology in the state we have come to recognise it during our relatively short life span compared to Earth systems time scales is likely to be futile and foolhardy.

That is not to say, we should be careless with our world and ignore our potential impact on the Earth's ecology. But we have to be balanced ourselves in our responses to the changes that may be taking place.

Where we are causing major and sudden disruptions to ecologies that have been a long time in the making, we ought to stop and think about the impact we are likely to cause. If on balance we can achieve our goals of survival and growth with less disruption, then we must do so. It would be just as foolhardy for us not to.

Cutting down some of the rain forests for our reasonable use in a sustainable manner is sensible. However, wiping out whole regions of rain forest and at such speed is seriously damaging and should be halted.

Sustainable fishing within the world's oceans is reasonable, but scouring huge sections of the ocean's sea beds with massive indiscriminate fishing nets is seriously damaging and should be halted.

Burning some fossil fuels to satisfy our survival and

growth needs, as a small portion of our total energy use that is mostly from renewable sources, is reasonable especially if we minimise atmospheric and water sources pollution.

A few strategic nuclear power plants for baseline energy needs in very few locations around the world is reasonable, especially if strict controls are applied to minimise their environmental pollution and remove any likely potential of accidental release of nuclear radiation.

In the end, we need to approach our world with sensitivity and realism. It is a region of balance that we must reach within our human societies where a combination of destruction and creation come together in a balance, means a sustainable environmental future.

Now that we recognise the Whole Earth as an ecological system that affects us no matter where we are around the world, it becomes obvious that we cannot cause damage in a remote part of the world and expect not to feel its impact.

Generating damaging pollutants in one part of the world and dumping them in another is not a solution to preventing ecological damage. Such damage will always be global, causing overall imbalances, no matter where it occurs.

However, there is only so much humanity can do to influence nature's balances. Many of the forces of nature are beyond our immediate understanding and certainly beyond our capacity to influence them.

We would be advised to have sufficient flexibility in our

existence and in our approach to the world around us so we can adapt to the changing world around us.

It is wise to remember that nature embodied in the Earth's ecosystem will prepare its own responses to the intrusion of a growing humanity and the increasing strain that this places on the Earth's systems. If we exceed sustainable boundaries, it is ourselves that suffer.

In the end, it is the Earth's systems that have the final say and humanity will be constrained one way or the other through the responses the Earth will throw back at us, be that rising sea levels, hurricanes, tsunamies, avalanches, earth quakes, volcanic eruptions, floods, famine, drought or other naturally occurring events.

The inflexibility of dinosaurs and their lack of ability to adapt led to their extinction.

On a positive note, humanity's resilience and ability to cope with nature's changes that are beyond our control will ensure our survival in one form or another.

THE NANNY STATE

In a system where the "Nanny State" takes the power for appropriate decision making away from the individual, the "State" effectively takes the responsibility for maintaining the points of balance within that system.

The "Nanny State" then invests so much energy into deciding what points of balance to exercise and to enforce. These choices may be achievable for a simple system with a single input, but very few systems if any are simple. This means that any decisions the "Nanny State" makes are likely to be at best bad compromises, and at worst, never appropriate for any one set of circumstances that may prevail.

Furthermore, by not empowering individuals to make their own guided but free decisions, it creates an oppressive atmosphere that feeds repulsion and a rebellious attitude amongst individuals. This in itself creates a never ending cycle of oppression as the "Nanny State" then takes on more responsibility for protecting its citizens from the "rogue elements" in society that it partially created by its own approach.

Individuals do not feel responsible for their actions. Their individual sense of "right and wrong" is then aimed at judging the "Nanny State" and the points of balance it has set.

With little or no feelings of personal responsibility, some individuals may become preoccupied with breaking the "Nanny State" rules where they believe it has put them at a disadvantage.

Then, the "Nanny State" has to invest even more energy and resources into law enforcement to sustain the position it has itself created.

Worse still, when the law enforcement catches up with those who broke the rules set by the "Nanny State", the justice system almost feels sympathy for those individuals who broke the rules.

Because the "Nanny State" takes so much of the authority away from individuals, the justice system becomes biased towards showing so much leniency to "guilty" individuals that the purpose for this justice system becomes questionable and the whole system of balances becomes ineffective.

Prescribed points of balance as those advocated by a "Nanny State", remove individual authority, reduce personal responsibility for the decisions and consequently reduce the individual's feelings of guilt associated with their actions.

JUSTICE SYSTEM

Justice is generally served when the scales are re-balanced in the eyes and hearts of society and more significantly in the eyes and hearts of those individuals most affected by the crime, the injustice and the imbalance.

If a "wrong" action is possible to be reversed without residual consequences or can be sufficiently re-balanced by a "right" action alone, then a "restorative justice" system may be sufficient and should be used.

It is likely that, only accidental "wrong" actions with no consequential permanent damage and with no injury caused could be addressed by a "restorative justice" system alone.

Whenever "restorative justice" is not sufficient or appropriate to restore the balance, re-balancing the scales of justice will inevitably involve some kind of retribution.

The nature and level of retribution required must in essence fit the injustice performed, but more importantly, the injustice experienced by those individuals most affected by the injustice.

This is the reason why all injustices must have retributions attached to them. Some must have a minimum retribution not to go below, others must have a maximum retribution not to be exceeded, while others still, must have retributions that lie between a minimum limit and a maximum limit.

For the scales of justice to ensure that injustices are not enacted during this re-balancing process itself, any maximum retribution needs to be automatically applied for that kind of injustice that is experienced. The justice system should then leave room for this level of retribution to be reduced or commuted down by those most affected by the injustice. In general, those are the victim, the family of the victim, the local community of the victim, then the rest of society.

However, when a retribution is reduced, it must not be commuted down below any minimum that has been accepted and pre-attached as appropriate for that injustice.

Serious as well as mild but persistently repeat offenders who ignore self-restraint, have to be readily, severely but justly dealt with in the interest of maintaining the balances needed for a harmonious society.

On the other hand, damaged individuals with psychological and / or mentally debilitating problems that prevent them from exercising self-restraint, need to be closely and constantly supervised and helped to ensure their own protection and the safety of the society around them from themselves.

EXPECTATIONS AND LOSS OF BALANCE

In the normal course of everyday living, we naturally, unconsciously and constantly weigh events and outcomes against our own perceived expectations.

The greater are our expectations, the more weight we attach to a particular outcome of a particular event and the greater is our feeling of disappointment when those expectations are not met.

When a number of events that have impact on our lives result in outcomes that are far away from our expectations, the extent of those differentials and the frequency of those unfavourable outcomes will contribute to uneasy feelings in an individual.

Consciously or unconsciously, we may start to attribute our accumulating disappointments to a "loss of balance".

We may recognise the events that are associated with our mounting disappointments to stem from or are connected with a common source, such as a particular individual, organisation or government. They inevitably become the focal point of our natural efforts to try and readdress the perceived loss of balance.

On a large scale, there are certain expectations that we all have, as human beings, that reflect our basic needs to exist and function at all. Food, shelter, warmth and security rank high amongst these. There are natural basic minimum levels for those expectations below which our ability to exist and function is jeopardised.

Genuine Poverty, Destitution and Famine are typical examples below our basic expectations of fundamental needs and are immediately and obviously recognised by all of us as a loss of balance that must be addressed.

Similarly but less critically and less consistently, on a small scale, every individual consciously or unconsciously have their own expectations about events that surround their own lives. These levels of expectations are partly instinctive but largely learnt through observation and previous experiences they accumulate from their daily lives.

The greater that is our ease of access to materials and resources around us, the greater is our expectation that these materials and resources should be available to us when we want them or need them and the greater is our disappointment when they are not.

Therefore, we may conclude that in the majority of situations where we may have felt disappointment at a particular outcome for a small-scale event, this was self-inflicted by the level of expectation we, ourselves, have set for it.

Since we are sentient beings with a large degree of control over our thoughts and decisions, an awareness of our own expectations and how they affect us, may help us manage them better to moderate the levels of expectations to be more appropriate to the events.

A poignant example is Poverty.

The dictionary definition of Poverty may be the condition of being without adequate food and money, a condition of scarcity of basic needs to ensure continued survival. That is what we would like to describe as "Genuine Poverty".

However, "Poverty" is often nowadays referred to in the context of not having the financial resources to buy all the modern day gadgets that those individuals desire to have and expect to have when they compare themselves to their peers. This is more about the individual's small-scale expectations rather than "Genuine Poverty".

Managing expectations on an individual, group or even national levels is essential and very helpful in avoiding accumulations of these small-scale disappointments that collectively may be perceived as a "loss of balance".

It is the perceived loss of balance and the perceived degree of imbalance that trigger the natural tendencies within ourselves to try and readjust the balance and to take actions to address the perceived source of that imbalance.

Some but not all small-scale riots and some teenage gang violence may be attributed to such perceived loss of balance resulting from collective accumulations of low-level disappointments that are themselves the result of not meeting individuals' own perceived expectations. When the perceived loss of balance is attached to an individual, a group or an organisation, they become the target for venting-off and for any retribution demanded by the perceived injustice.

In addition, disappointment itself is a negative emotion that most individuals would prefer not to experience. Therefore, managing small-scale expectations is also helpful at maintaining a greater degree of happiness or less unhappiness in our daily lives. This is a contributing factor to our perception of the "quality of life" we experience.

To take the example of a farming family that lives in a remote rural region where they are self-sufficient and secure, compared with a family that lives in a large metropolitan modern city. Both families may be living comfortably and contentedly in their own surroundings. However, their expectations of ease of access and speed of access to services in their area are tempered by their own experiences that are vastly different.

ADDICTIONS

As previously described, cumulatively, failing to meet small-scale expectations leads to disappointments that may collectively be perceived as a loss of balance that needs to be addressed.

Most individuals accept their duty and their ability to manage their own expectations under normal conditions, even if many find that difficult to achieve.

We all make decisions every day, from the mundane to the profound, we make judgements and choices.

Even when our choices are apparently made freely, big issues or small decisions, they are often constrained by our abilities, resources and the limitations imposed upon us by our peers, our society and the governing laws.

Individuals making their choices and decisions with free will and in total control of their faculties, are likely to make the choices that will maintain the balance they expect to have in their own lives.

However, an addict is an individual with some form of dependency. This dependency will drive the individual to take whatever action they need to satisfy the dependency. Even though such actions may be in the end detrimental to the interests of that individual.

An addiction is itself a manifestation of a state of imbalance, but worse still, it drives the individual to a further state of imbalance.

As clearly recognised, an addict is unlikely to make the choices that will bring balance back to their lives. Their dependency presents them with a skewed view of their true needs. The addiction becomes the overriding priority that must be satisfied.

Therefore, an addict's decisions cannot be relied upon to be constructive or effective in creating a balance for the individual or for society. Their addiction is self-fulfilling. In the majority, they are unable to recognise it or do anything to change it should they recognise it.

The addict needs help. The cycle of addiction has to be broken.

Since an addict will not freely exercise the necessary self-restraint to overcome the addiction, they need direct help in doing just that. This help often comes in the shape of family and friends. But if this is not forthcoming, society has to act on their behalf through the prevailing laws.

From a wider perspective, addiction comes in many shapes and sizes.

Mostly, addiction is associated with substance dependency, from the low-level addictions to mild drinks of Coffee and Tea all the way to addictions to potent drugs like Cocaine and powerful alcoholic drinks.

But addiction can also be to a particular behaviour, a situation, an individual, an object …..etc.
For example, watching TV, a violent partner or playing a computer game.

To restore the state of balance necessary, decisions have to be made on behalf of the addict to help the addict and often without their consent.

Authority may have to be exercised in the interest of the addict, against their will, in line with consensus that has to be reached by individuals suited to make such decisions relevant to the individual and the prevailing circumstances.

Such authority should be exercised until the addict is safely capable of making their own self-conscious judgements and decisions, in the interest of maintaining an appropriate balance once again.

In extreme cases of seriously damaging addiction, control may have to be totally removed from an individual over their movements, access to the sources of their addiction, and their liberty to make their own choices while they are under the influence of their addiction.

Because of the controversial nature of exercising significant authority over an individual's life, such decisions and actions must only be made by trained specialists and be legally approved on a case by case basis by local judicial powers.

Once the influence of the addiction has been removed from the individual's ability to make appropriate choices, their rights to full control over their lives and their own actions must be fully restored.

DOMINANCE
AND ITS ACCOMPANIED DESPAIR

Our search for adequate points of balance is often in itself the result of a loss of balance.

The balance we need for a stable set of balances that we can rely on in our daily lives, for our moral code, psychological well-being and physiological interactions with the world around us.

A loss or doubt about what are appropriate and commonly accepted points of balance, raises the levels of individual's tensions, elevates individual's and society's anxieties, results in distrust, disappointment, hyper-tension and potential despair.

These are all factors that contribute to consequential events where outbursts of conflicts flare up that are not easily predicted.

There have been many examples during the 20th Century where small pockets of conflict and unrest have arisen in modern societies without immediately obvious causes. Some of these may be attributed to a loss or doubt about points of balance.

Whenever individuals or groups who are in some position of power exceed the level of their authority, as it is perceived by the majority of those under their influence, for the purposes of accentuating their position of dominance and to further their own self-interests at the expense of that majority, a sense of oppression is created.

Historically, oppressive dictatorships arise from a psychological need for dominance. Very often driven by individual or group feelings of their own inadequacy or insecurity, but on occasion by pure greed and self-interest at the expense of others.

Such dictatorships are not interested in sustainable balance but go out of their way to preserve their positions by attempting to increase the bias towards their own self-preservation and the preservation of their dominance, and consequently increase the imbalance further.

This is what could be described as the self-perpetuating "Psychology of Dominance".

Such "Psychology of Dominance" can be observed at many levels. From dysfunctional relationships between partners or within families, to playground behaviours of child bullying, to local authorities justifying questionable decisions, to national governments imposing draconian laws, all the way to autocratic rulers who gained position through exercise of military power or violence.

The natural order demands that balance is restored, and the more extreme the "Psychology of Dominance", the greater the oppression it engenders amongst those under its influence.

As the oppression escalates and normal efforts to stand-up to it are quashed by it, a feeling of despair and depression spreads amongst those affected by the oppression.

Strangely though, most living animal creatures on this earth appear to have a built-in defence mechanism that comes into effect in extreme states of despair. It is often observed when an animal is trapped and cornered with no apparent path out of the danger that has befallen it. In such situations, most animals are prepared to and will fight to destruction rather surrender to their desperate fate.

Human individuals and societies appear to exhibit a similar kind of reaction when faced with the despair of an extremely oppressive situation. They are prepared to put aside their normal instincts of self-preservation and will stand-up to the oppression even if it means their own destruction. That is what we can describe as the reactive "Psychology of Despair".

'The child that stand-up to the bully, risking life and limb. The battered wife or husband standing up to their partner risking life or limb.
The unauthorised demonstrators in a police state, risking life and limb.
The armed revolutionary movement facing an oppressive military dictatorship, risking being ostracised and obliterated.'
These are some of the many examples that can be recounted.

Take one example. Many a revolution in human history can be attributed to this "Psychology of Despair" where whole peoples or nations have risen and united in armed revolution against their perceived oppressors.

History is littered with examples where masses of people feeling a serious loss of balance in their lives join revolutionary movements and grasp the first ideology they can find that appears to provide them with salvation and the hope to readdress the imbalance the are experiencing.

Generally, human individuals have a need to believe that a suitable system must exist that will offer them a set of balances to make their lives better and happier.

How often though, have revolutions offered panaceas that were quickly found by the populations that adopted them to be "wrong" or incomplete.

Frequently, these revolutionary movements are focused on readdressing some particular imbalance in their populations, often at the expense of other balances that they either disregard as not important or do not recognise at all.

The drive of such a revolutionary movement to readdress the particular imbalance is so strong and determined that they often over-shoot the "region of balance" for this particular element to excess in the opposite direction. This initiates what many describe as a "Pendulum effect".

Similarly but less obviously, the "Psychology of Despair" drives some individuals to sacrifice their lives in individual acts that they believe they had to do. Like a hunted animal that is cornered, their "Psychology of Despair" does not leave them any path out of their perceived predicament. Rather than succumb to their perceived fate, those individuals will attempt to destroy the source of the threat against them even if they end their own lives in the process.

This could possibly explain the psychology of the "suicide bomber". However, sadly, most such acts appear ill judged and often ineffectual in restoring any balance. Worse still, in many cases, such acts feed any perceived oppressors with additional reasons to further their own oppression.

THE PENDULUM EFFECT

As described in another section of this book, for a system to balance effectively and in a stable manner, there needs to be a choice for an appropriate region of balances within which various factors and inputs are constantly nudging each other.

While these factors and inputs remain within their own regions of balances, the whole system remains stable and the complex interactions between the relevant regions of balances demand a minimum of effort and attention to maintain the system stability.

For each of these factors or inputs, its region of balance could be described as the acceptable region where the pendulum would swing and is nudged from both directions to maintain its swing.

If the pendulum is nudged too strongly in one direction, the swing of the pendulum could be increased to exceed the accepted region of swing (region of balance) and over-shoot to cause damage to its surrounding environment. When this situation affects other balances in a system, it could result in system instability.

When a particular region of balance for a particular factor is over-shot, the natural tendency of individuals is to re-adjust the balance by applying various pressures on this factor or input to nudge it back in the opposite direction.

When adjustments are appropriate and of the appropriate strength or magnitude, the pendulum swings back but stays within the appropriate region of balance. This is the pendulum effect operating naturally and effectively.

However, if the nudges or adjustments in the opposite direction are judged incorrectly and are too strong, the pendulum swings back but over-shoots the region of balance in the opposite direction. Similarly creating an imbalance on the other side that may be even further away from the required region of balance.

To correct the new imbalance, nudges or adjustments need to be made towards the original direction. But again these nudges need to be applied correctly and with the correct strength. And so it goes on until the pendulum is comfortably swinging within its appropriate region of balance with the minimum energy it needs and deserves.

How often have the oppressed become the oppressors and the abused have become the abusers. This statement is not intended to justify such actions, only to explain them from the perspective of a pendulum swing. Individuals are still culpable and responsible for their actions that are ultimately under their own control. By their careful and responsible actions individuals can avert the pendulum effect and restore the region of balance.

CULTURE CLASHES
OF THE 20TH CENTURY

In times before the industrial revolution and the advent of faster transportation systems that were eventually followed by the instant communication systems we have become familiar with, the world was made up of relatively clearly-bounded communities that only interacted through adjoining land boundaries and through very slow trade routes.

The relatively secluded human communities enjoyed a pace of life that represented the demands of those times and those environments. Each community evolved their own culture to suit those demands and those environments.

Cultures only interacted through trade or conflict that arose at adjoining land boundaries often resulting in wars of different magnitudes. Whenever that happened historically, any resulting culture clash was often only between two sides. Any bicultural clash was then resolved through one culture totally being replaced or partially being absorbed into the other culture and then new points of balances being developed gradually for the altered societies and the new environments they faced.

Nowadays, faster transportation methods have made international migration easier. More still, instant communication systems and the spread of the internet have resulted in the intermingling of human societies through cultural migration, migration of thoughts and instant exchanges of information and emotional states across the world.

The human societies represented by individuals from all over the world bring with them their own sets of points of balance, which to each of them are likely to be appropriate but to the new mix may not be appropriate.

Whether we recognise our inevitable need or not for our harmony to reach new common sets of points of balances, the various cultures that historically existed almost separately around the world are now coming together into the 21st century with multiple crescendos of cultures clashing.

The opening up of long closed cultures and the exposure of the mixes of beliefs, national and individual self-interests, and differing ideologies are demonstrated by the observed conflicts of all magnitudes arising at most points where these mixes are coming together, from the next-door neighbours to the international face-offs that have no physical boundaries to the etherial world of the Internet.

These conflicts are the results of points of balances, that originally evolved to suit particular environments and circumstances, being exposed to suddenly changed parameters that they are not necessarily appropriate for or suited to deal with.

This recognition is inevitably our first step towards reaching new points of balances that suit the changed world that is evolving.

It is also part of this transitional loss of balance that proponents of certain ideologies and groups and nations that hold the prevailing balance of military, financial or ideological power over others, will try to impose their own self-interests on what they regard the new points of balances should be. What some may refer to as "The New World Order".

What some of these proponents, groups and nations may not recognise is that by their own attempts to impose their own will so forcibly, they are likely to push the pendulum beyond its region of balance and consequently generate an opposing reaction that will be equal or be of greater strength. By doing so, they are actually undermining the representation of their own inputs into the new regions of balance that are needed to be reached.

And so, the pendulum will swing. And the greater the push, the greater the swing!

THE MIDDLE-EAST

A prevailing international perspective of the early 21st Century would pick out several pockets of conflict around the world. Probably the most obvious is that of the Middle-East. From Israel and Palestine to the Gulf wars and Iraq, to Iran, Afghanistan and Pakistan, the Middle-East is a complex example of self-interests driving the pendulum swing beyond its regions of balance.

The historical exercise of power politics driven by the economic gain and self-interest related to Oil Reserves across the whole of the region further increased the strategically important role of the Middle-East in determining the points of balances in the "New World Order" of the 20th and 21st Centuries.

This led to the manipulations of governments across the region particularly exemplified by the regime of the Shah in Iran.

Further manipulations through direct and indirect military exploits, again across the region but particularly exemplified by the Israel-Palestine-Lebanon land occupations.

Then, partly as a consequence of the pendulum swing in one direction, then the other, and then back again, the recent Gulf-wars, the Iraq war and the wars waged in Afghanistan and Pakistan.

In hind-sight, we may recognise the effect of the creation of the state of Israel and the repeated violations of the rights of the Palestinian people on the psychology of individuals that consider themselves members of the same larger Middle-East family. This situation was compounded by the repeated and continued land occupations and land appropriations in Palestine and at the borders of the surrounding countries.

We could consider this initial severe pendulum push. The reaction to that pendulum swing was initially localised to the immediately affected region. But, as the imbalance that was created, resulted in perpetually worsening conditions for individuals and countries in the region, the reaction to the imbalance mounted in strength and galvanised individuals and groups to form resistance movements such as the PLO. Also, wars were waged by the immediate Arab countries against Israel in the 1970's with limited effects.

However, the push from the other direction represented by the military and psychological support offered to Israel by the USA nullified the initial reactive push against Israel and pushed the pendulum back.

The power exercised by the USA and Israel in the region now included manipulations of local governments to circumvent further organised border wars against Israel. That is likely to have increased the feelings of oppression amongst the local and wider affected populations. The governments that represented them became impotent at removing the oppression they perceived was being exercised against them.

As the need persisted to push the pendulum back, the means available to those who were feeling the perceived oppression became limited. However, the natural need to push the pendulum back cannot be made to vanish. Consequently, those feeling the perceived oppression devised new means to push the pendulum back.

Sadly, with legitimate means of resistance and pushing back being denied to them, some individuals started to resort to illegitimate means and methods that would normally be unacceptable to those individuals themselves. The "Psychology of Despair" was initiated. Abductions and Hijacks followed by the "Suicide Bomber" started to be used.

The rallying cry of the only unifying force in the Middle-East that is unaffected by politics or political boundaries or any social and tribal allegiances became the channel to galvanise resistance and the push of the pendulum that is necessary to readjust the balance.

The moderate message of Islam like other widely adopted world religions revolves around a set of balances aimed at creating harmony and happiness for its followers. Looking at the core values of the religion of Islam and its scriptures, it clearly advocates moderation and rejects damaging acts such as terrorism, as the majority of Islam's followers would confirm.

As the perceived oppression persisted and accentuated, those without other means of resistance looked to other muslims. They needed to convince others to follow the only means of subversive resistance that they felt was available to them. And like others before them, they used the justification of divine authority to give legitimacy to their actions.

Islamic fundamentalist extremism was born. The leaders of these fundamentalist groups looked to the islamic scriptures. They took extracts that were not meant to be interpreted in isolation, used the instructions out of the context they were intended for and moulded new distorted messages that would normally be unpalatable to muslims but that acted as a pressure relief to the muslim masses. Many moderate muslims must have felt an urge to turn a blind eye to this.

Equally but perhaps less extreme at the time, the oppression felt by Iranians as a result of the exploits of the Shah who was supported by the USA, spawned the Iranian Islamic Revolution.

Unfortunately, the extremists message did not remain on the margins. Support for the extremists' message amongst muslims was growing on the back of the continuing perceived feelings of oppression that was pervaded by the continued support for Israel and its violating actions in the region. The normally unacceptable message of the extremists' did not only spread, but amongst certain groups, it also became more extreme. Al-Qaeda was born.

The extremists' groups like "Al-Qaeda" have no government to manipulate, they have no specific land with borders to wage war against and they do not have one executive leader to assassinate. These extremists have found a way to push the pendulum back that may be effective.

Unfortunately, having been spawned as a consequence of the imbalance forced upon the Middle-East and then subsequently through removing all legitimate means to restore the balance, the actions of these extremists even though effective in pushing back, they are likely to push back beyond the region of balance in the opposite direction and therefore perpetuate the pendulum swing back and forth.

Worse still, the influence of these extremists is also spreading around the world, their push of the pendulum has itself initiated imbalances in other parts of the world. From Malaysia to Somalia to Europe to the USA to Pakistan and Afghanistan, just to mention a few.

It is certain that the extremists are not the solution to restoring the balance. They are merely a by-product of a situation and are likely to fade away if the situation that spawned them no longer exists.

To believe that balance would be restored by quashing or destroying these extremist groups is also foolhardy.

If the reasons that spawned those extremist groups still remain, then it will be inevitable that new extremist groups, possibly more extreme in their actions will be created to readdress the even greater imbalance.

Balance can only be restored in the Middle-East if the source of the imbalance is addressed and resolved legitimately in a way that will remove the perceived feelings of oppression amongst all the populations of the region and their wider family world wide. It is also the means to remove the reason-de-être for the extremists, especially in the eyes and hearts of those most affected by the imbalance, namely, the downtrodden populations of the region.

A good start for reducing the imbalance in the eyes of the Palestinian people and their larger Middle East family may be for the USA to halt its unconditional support for Israel so that appropriate pressures could be applied on both sides to follow through with fair and open negotiations.

The objective in the end has to be a fair settlement that would give the downtrodden Palestinian people rights to their legitimate lands, to allow them to create their own genuine state and afford them the freedoms and opportunities that all of us would expect for ourselves.

Since it is accepted that Israel with its long standing ally, the USA, hold the balance of military power, only such a position that would return to the Palestinians the respect and dignity of a free peoples is likely to be seen by the Palestinians and others as having redressed most if not all of the imbalance.

No doubt, there will be many complexities throughout any process towards reaching such a position, the greatest and most difficult of all is the question of who has jurisdiction over the holy city of Jerusalem.

When positions that are diametrically polarised are so entrenched from all sides of the negotiating table regarding a particular issue, there are only two possible ways forward. Either to end the negotiations and any hope of resolving the problem, or to bypass the area of difficulty by finding a separate neutral solution for it that is not in favour of any of the negotiating participants.

To that end, it may be necessary to consider the possibility of removing Jerusalem from the jurisdiction of any particular party or state.

Perhaps, it may be fitting that a city which is so revered by so many people should become an international city-state that is self-governing and not be under any other jurisdiction.

Israel already has a sense of security for its people. What is missing, to attempt a re-balance, is for Palestine to develop a similar sense of security for its people.

FROM REVOLUTIONS TO EMPIRES COLLAPSING

A balance in a system that is constantly being manipulated and changed is very difficult to achieve, and if achieved, it is not easy to maintain and sustain without a constant determined effort.

As evident by our history of human society, where individuals, groups and nations are constantly changing the world around them, our unrestrained actions often result in destruction and oppression as well as the opportunities they were intended to create.

In the case of 'Revolution' mounting, as previously described. It is often the consequence of a loss of balance generated by a single distorting action or multiple actions and their perceived oppression. A significant blow initiating a sudden and serious push of the pendulum within a group or a nation, that requires a corrective reactive push in the opposite direction.

Such a situation arising from one single adverse event could be referred to as a "Cataclysmic event".

A first and significant imbalance initiated by a "Cataclysmic event" is not always a fast acting effect over a short time scale.

It is possible that a "Cataclysmic event" could be a single significant but small event that gradually builds up its influence over a period of time but then seriously accelerates its push in one direction that results in significantly over-shooting the acceptable region of balance.

An example of this for a particular population or nation could be, an external national or corporate power imposing its influence on free-elections or installing puppet governments in an apparently stable region of the world to gain favour for some specific interests at the expense of other balances.

However, history has other examples of balances lost that took a different form and generated a different type of reactive push of the pendulum.

Whether we are considering "National" empires or "Corporate" empires, historically, we could describe empires that evolved in response to the prevailing regional balances in resources and the readiness of the local populations to use or in many cases to exploit those resources.

Most fledgling empires are started by groups or nations wishing to bolster their ability to survive, initially in a defensive manner to repel external adversaries, but then going on to bolster their position by offensive action to destroy or absorb what they perceived to be potential threats to their positions.

As empires expand, the sets of balances they grew to control and maintain change. The absorption of larger groups or organisations brings with it internal conflicts of interest, conflicts of perceived points of balance within the now growing empire.

A fledgling empire is able to focus all its resources on those external factors and threats it considers necessary to control or remove. Just like a modern dictatorship, the empire feels a right to exercise its growing power over all those it dominates. Creating much perceived oppression in the process.

However, unlike a dictatorship, an empire is able to absorb those whom it oppresses into its own fold and turn them into citizens or members that do its bidding.

But every individual the empire brings into its fold changes the empire by bringing their own sets of balances and self-interests into the core of empire.

As empires consequently grow, some conscious but many unconscious balances are affected and altered. Achieving new balances or maintaining existing balances become increasingly difficult.

Recognising what re-balances are needed for the internal stability of empire becomes more clouded and more difficult to identify.

Empire expands further. Its internal system of balances gradually drifts out of balance. Empire degenerates, as is easily seen in hindsight. But there is often no internal pendulum swing. The imbalances created within the empire, eating away at its core and causing it to crumble, often do not meet with a response from its citizens or members.

In the absence of a democratic structure that allows for modifying influences that would change the direction of empire, those in charge of directing the empire continue their actions undeviating.

However, the individuals in charge of that empire are not always aware of its state of decay, they often believe that they are enjoying the spoils and decadent rewards of their positions of power that they believe they rightly deserve.

History is full of such examples of empire. Whether it is empires of nations or empires of business.

Recorded human history of nation empires that demonstrate this effect, includes the Persian empire, the Greek empire, the Roman empire, the British empire and the Russian empire amongst many more.

Also, modern corporate history of business empires is littered with businesses of varying sizes reflecting the same conditions and responses, with similar conclusions. The most prominent of which is the case of the 'Lehman Brothers' banking empire that collapsed spectacularly in 2008, causing a world-wide credit crunch and a deep recession.

As empires weaken, the pendulum push back swing often comes from outside the empire, not from within.

The external forces that empire previously controlled start to gather strength to repel their perceived oppressive power of the empire.

Eventually, empire collapses, breaks up and often gets absorbed into new empires in the making. And so the cycle repeats. And history repeats itself.

DEMOCRACIES AND BALANCE

The causes of a first position that is reached outside a region of balance, could be the result of many small cumulative nudges being more in one direction than the other over a long period of time.

Often, this is normal and can be carefully corrected. However, sometimes, the very small incremental nudges towards imbalance are difficult to perceive and to be recognised until the end effect of imbalance has been reached.

As the recorded and pre-recorded history of human interactions goes back some time. Those interactions that required social and geopolitical balances also frequently go back some time. It is sometimes difficult to recognise when the first position of imbalance was reached and what were its specific causes.

None-the-less, whether it is a first imbalance or the imbalance reached by subsequent swings of the pendulum leading to the present, an active system, left to its own devices, will attempt to readjust its own balance.

In democratic structures, where members of an organisation or the people of a nation recognise the growing imbalance and the drift towards imbalance, this is often dealt with by re-election of ruling panels, boards of directors, governments, prime-ministers or presidents.

Those re-elected are often from a persuasion of the opposite side of the centre, in a natural attempt by the system to readdress the balance.

SOCIO-ECONOMIC LIBRALISM OF THE 20ᵀᴴ CENTURY

The 1960's brought about an era of what many would describe as socio-economic liberalism that also brought with it many changes in expected human behaviours.

In the aftermath of two world wars that were themselves extreme swings of the pendulum that had to take place to correct imbalances created on a world-wide scale by preceding events. The two world wars destroyed nations and communities, altered societies and their perceived points of balances and created expectations of new regions of balances.

Accompanied by the continuing and rapidly advancing technologies, many of which were driven by the demands of the instabilities prevailing during the world wars periods, the 1950s and 1960s were a cross-road for societies broken, having lost direction and previously established balances.

Irrespective of winners and losers, the two world wars were two major clashes amongst human societies with self-interests that created transient allegiances and pushed our world almost to the point of self-destruction. As established balances were undermined, the pendulum swings became extremely destructive.

The 1960s was an era where humanity was attempting to heal itself and find new points of balance in the altered world that was then prevailing.

With few remaining accepted points of balance and few groups within human society that were sufficiently unaffected by the events during the world wars, the continuity of previous systems of balances was broken in many regions around the world. No more so than the focal points of the conflicts, starting with Europe.

The natural tendency to apply self-restraint to maintain accepted and expected regions of balance had been weakened by the large scale loss of balance and the loss of human close-knit family units and close-knit communities that traditionally reinforced the need for self-restraint to maintain the expected regions of balance.

With diminished self-restraint, many individuals acted on their pure self-interest and personal desires, in many cases with total disregard to others and with disregard to any harm they may be causing.

To satisfy a growing demand for those personal desires, industry and commerce, fuelled by new and improving technologies, responded with great enthusiasm to the potential of making massive profits driven by unrestrained natural human emotions including greed for materialism and desire for power.

Slick advertising methods followed by efficient Sales and Marketing techniques were created by industry and commerce to sustain customers' demands for their products and services.

Intrinsic to those advertising campaigns and sales and marketing techniques was a careful and clever manipulation of the psychology of human populations to drive their desires further to buy the products flooding the markets.

Customers responded as expected. Their desires overwhelming, new "religions" were being created. The "religions" of Commercialism and Consumerism were spreading across the world.

The social "norms" that were accepted regions of balances by previous generations of human societies started to be rejected and challenged. New "norms" were being sought based on a reducing sense of self-restraint.

Individuals started to crave unheeded self-gratification with all the damaging imbalance that comes with it.

Worse still, a growing determination towards instant gratification meant that individuals desire to "Live for the day" and to "Take what you can now!" represented an expectation for entitlement with no corresponding expectation to give back.

"If it is there, I want to take it!"….
Theft became justifiable and desirable. No recognition of the recklessness of such attitude and behaviours.

Amongst many groups of individuals, crime became accepted and expected. A readiness to break laws was becoming seen as a sign of strength, and the refusal to partake in such criminal activity as a sign of weakness.

Organised crime became more sophisticated and more widespread.

A consumer driven crime wave in countries like the UK started around the mid 1950s and grew into the remainder of the 20th century.

CRIME AND SOCIETY

There will always be individuals who are inclined to and intent on doing what they want with little or no self-restraint at the expense of others.

Such individuals are essentially destructive, no matter how falsely and positively they may wish to promote themselves, and no matter how they may be admired and idolised by others for their portrayed charisma or questionable deeds.

Societies have suffered such individuals throughout history. Their actions creating many imbalances and resulting in reactions that were needed to deal with these individuals and the consequences of their actions to the societies around them.

These individuals are resistant to the idea of conforming to any systems of balances that do not give them advantage over others and they are not interested in the principle of self-restraint towards achieving a harmonious society.

Intent on their own self-interests irrespective, these individuals seek power, manipulate others and alter the laws to create unbalanced systems of enforcement that bolster their own positions.

It may be possible to recognise well-known individuals such as Adolph Hitler and Mussolini in such a category.

However, such individuals exist at all levels of society. Examples include serial killers, fraudsters and organised criminals.

The only means of re-addressing the balance against such determined criminal elements whether in local society or on the scale of world society is by collective severe sanctions, the rule of law and judicial retribution.

For other individuals in society, crime is more the result of passing temptations that is preventable through the exercise of self-restraint.

From a violent or violating reaction to a particular situation, to the opportunistic theft, to the damage caused by carelessness, such crimes should be addressed through a combination of instilling clear boundaries with careful guidance and nurturing alongside an efficient justice system that also provides an element of deterrence.

In societies like the UK, in the early part of this 21st century, there is an increased fear of crime and criminals.

This could be attributed in part to the easier and quicker forms of news coverage that nowadays deliver knowledge of crimes at such a speed with such a frequency that it may distort perceptions about any changing patterns in the frequency of crimes.

Similarly, the reporting of violent crime in much detail is also likely to heighten the sense of fear of crime amongst the general public.

This fear of crime has been used to justify the extensive and intrusive use of CCTV systems, even to private areas where they would not have been acceptable previously.

CCTV does not prevent crimes but sometimes helps to catch criminals. By definition, it is not the solution to the problem of crime. It merely attempts to compensate for inadequate law enforcement, and inadequate self-restraint.

However, law enforcement itself is not the solution to the general problem of crime. Although, on a psychological level it could contribute to a sense of deterrence that can affect levels of crime.

The true solution to any problem is always in finding the true causes and the major contributing factors that drive the problem to exist. Then to find ways to either remove the causes of the problem or minimise the effect of the major contributors to that problem.

By eliminating or reducing the causes of a problem, the problem would be removed or minimised and the need for any corresponding law enforcement reduced.

As described in a previous section of this book, an "Optimum System" requires minimum expenditures of resources and energy to maintain the regions of balance, leaving more capacity for genuine productive behaviours.

Crime is easily recognisable as a driver for imbalance and therefore must be dealt with. But not by concentrating on laws and law enforcement.

Our main focus has to be the causes of crime and how to eliminate or reduce them so that they become ineffectual.

At this point, what we may recognise as the causes of crime suddenly becomes open for a debate that could be distracting from the objective of our efforts.

To avoid such a distraction and dilution in focus, it is possible to categorise, classify and eliminate. Simple techniques to help us maintain our focus.

Crime may be categorised into two basic types:
      1 - Undeterred crime
      2 - Preventable crime

Crime as categorised by law enforcement is normally in relation to the seriousness of the crime. This is only useful to law enforcers who have to plan and provide appropriate resources to deal with the aftermath of a crime and catching the perpetrators.

No matter how we categorise crime, every member in society should have a clear duty and responsibility to protect the society they are part of.

This means that individual members of society who care about others, must never be risk averse to an extent that makes them averse to challenging those who are either determined to cause harm or those who are intent on hiding their crime or try to "get away with it".

Our categorisation, "Undeterred Crime" refers to determined, pre-meditated crime that is enacted by individuals who are not and will not be deterred by self-restraint, or by recognising the damage they cause to society nor by the efforts of law enforcement.

Irrespective of the seriousness of the consequences of the crime, this is the category described at the beginning of this chapter and how it can only be tackled by law enforcement and by judicial justice.

The causes of "Undeterred Crime" are the individuals who perpetrate the crime themselves. Law enforcement must be extremely focused and determined to apprehend such individuals no matter what is the seriousness of their crimes, so that they can be dealt with severely by an appropriate judicial justice system.

Whether small or large scale crimes, the consequences of "Undeterred Crimes", singularly or collectively over a period of time, are a significant source of imbalance and a serious cause of damage to society.

In comparison, all other crimes, whether their consequences are serious or not, they are enacted by individuals who should be able and willing to exercise reasonable self-restraint. Therefore, by definition, all these other crimes are "Preventable Crimes".

Fortunately, the majority of crimes are "Preventable Crimes".

Although attention will be required from law enforcement to deal with the aftermath of "Preventable Crime", the demand on law enforcement to deal with this type of crime should reduce if the preventable crimes are prevented and reduced, leaving greater resources to deal with the "Undeterred Crime".

So, how do we even start to attempt to reduce "Preventable Crime"?

The obvious answer is that it is not possible or appropriate to use law enforcement to reduce "Preventable Crime". These are preventable crimes because the individual should be capable of preventing them through exercising self-restraint.

Consequently, when referring to the causes of crime in this context, it is the causes that prevent self-restraint that must be addressed.

It is often the case that "Crime" is ascribed to "Poverty". If there exists evidence that crime levels are higher in poorer areas, that being the case, then it does not immediately infer that "Poverty" is a cause of crime. That is to say, because someone is poor, they should be more likely to enact a crime.

Any linkage between "Poverty" and crime is likely to be through the fact that some "Poorer" neighbourhoods came to exist through herding together large groups of under-privileged members of society who are treated as outcasts and do not feel a duty or belonging to the wider society.

It is this lack of inclusion and any aspirations of inclusion that maintains them on the margins of society and does not allow them to establish communities that are coherent and consistent with the societies they should be part of.

It is a myth that "poverty" is a cause of moral breakdown and a source of social degeneration.

It is sometimes suggested that there may be a link between the "Haves" and the "Have Nots" and the increased levels of crime in the UK in the early part of this 21st century.

To take a simple example of a small coherent village community anywhere in the world where the individual is valued for their contribution and the survival of the community depends on this contribution. Even though the average individual income in the community may be very small, the sense of belonging to the community and society in general is very well established. All the expected balances that minimise "Preventable Crime" are evident in the individuals' self-restrained behaviours.

A loss of the sense of community only leaves room for the "Me" world.

A "Me World" where self-gratification and self-interest are the main driving forces. A world where, even "Bad" becomes seen as good!.

Obviously, "Genuine Poverty" is an affront to the decency of human society and must be redressed.

Providing channels and opportunities out of a perpetual poverty cycle is a good and important thing to do. However, these will not necessarily improve society.

What is required is to help high-crime areas that are collectives of individuals deprived of inclusion and opportunities, to develop a sense of community and a sense of belonging to the wider society. To provide the individual with a sense that they are valued by the community and by society for any positive contribution they are willing to make.

Such an approach would develop and strengthen the individuals' sense of right and wrong and helps them find an appropriate region of balance between their rights and their responsibilities as they grow to recognise themselves as part of their communities and their larger society.

It is quoted that in the UK at the time of writing, "16 to 24 year olds, contribute increasing numbers and more horrific mindless unpredictable crimes than any other group in society". These could be referred to as "The Lost Youth".

What is happening to these "Lost Youths" that is putting them on the margins of society and making them rebel mindlessly against society?

A very deep question that can only be addressed by simplifying the situation to its basic elements.

Recognising the "mindless and unpredictable" nature of these crimes suggests that they are likely to be unplanned and unpremeditated. Therefore, in the majority, they are likely to be opportunistic "Preventable Crimes".

This suggests that such crimes are enacted because of the pure removal of all self-restraint from these individual youths.

How do we engender or even recover the loss of this self-restraint?

Self-restraint naturally exists within all of us. We exercise it automatically when we consciously or unconsciously believe an action will cause us direct or indirect harm. For example, most of us will not voluntarily stick our naked finger into a burning flame.

So, what is happening amongst these "Lost Youths" that is preventing them from applying their natural self-restraint to actions that harm others?

The clue may be that "others" is the key! It is possible that these "Lost" youths have no interest in other members of society and they no longer value others. Possibly because they are consciously or unconsciously reciprocating an emotion that others do not value them.

These "Lost" youths may be lost because they lost their sense of belonging to their communities and society and lost the sense that they could be valued members of society.

However, amongst a few "Lost" youths, their criminal acts may prove to be "Undeterred". This may be established after efforts have been exhausted to rehabilitate them. Law enforcement and the Judicial Justice system will need to deal with these individuals appropriately and severely.

When a child is born, they learn about the world around them through the eyes of those around them. Generally those are the parents of the child.

It actually takes a community to raise a child. The early years start with the parents but the process is continued and completed by the whole community and by society.

For a child to have grown into a "Lost" youth, the child rearing process has undoubtedly gone wrong. Starting with the family unit, then the local community and then society as a whole.

There is recent observable evidence that in some sections of society in the UK, parents are distancing themselves from their responsibilities and their duties to their children!

The family breakdown that was accentuated in the aftermath of the 2nd World War has gradually led us towards an increasingly broken society.

A child starts their early learning by copying those around them. Generally those are the parents. Then, the child is guided through the remainder of their development by their community, their school and their peers. The mixes of influences are very individual and they depend on personalities and circumstances.

In societies where the family unit is strong and is an established cornerstone of society, experience, knowledge and moral standings are passed through the generations by personal example, direct teachings, peer pressure and community expectations.

There is almost a sense that the world is still healing itself from the aftermath of the World Wars of the 20th century. The upheaval that destroyed communities and social structures, resulting in uncertain systems of balance for the emerging mixed societies is still a major factor in the current state of modern social incohesion at the start of the 21st century.

Throughout human history, many societies have found their balance after turmoil by a process of trial an error combined with some vision and good fortune.

It is as though today's youth, unwilling to be guided by the social structures that would normally provide them with the nurture and knowledge of appropriate regions of balance, many of today's youths are having to establish and re-learn the rights and wrongs the hard way. A broken society will eventually mend and will take time.

For those "Lost" youths, they represent a generation that has not managed to find appropriate boundaries of self-restraint that they are prepared to believe are to their own benefit.

Broken societies that lost their way in the past were on occasions helped by a dose of religious structure that provided guidance in the form of some basic clear-cut boundaries. A well-known example is "The Ten Commandments".

With these "Lost" youths, sanctions do not work, they are inclined to do whatever they want! A likely approach would need to make these youths "want" to change their behaviour. A process of rehabilitation is probably best. A helping hand providing opportunities alongside clear guidance.

It is difficult to be certain whether or not the "Lost" youth of today can be re-integrated into society.

However, if it is possible at all, this could only be achieved by showing them the advantages of self-restraint in their outward behaviour. Then, when an individual shows a willingness to partake in this process, a mutual relationship could be established with the rest of society that may recover the imbalance.

TO REHABILITATE
THOSE "LOST" YOUTHS

On a practical level; to complete the process of integration into society, these individuals need to believe they are valued members of society.

One possible way to achieve that could be:
- to identify their individual strengths and weaknesses
- find out what their interests are
- then reconcile their interests and strengths
- recognise a possible activity they could carry out that
    would be of value to society and that they recognise
    they enjoy and that other members of society
    appreciate.

If such a suitable pursuit can be identified and an existing local opportunity can be found for that individual to join, the rehabilitation process is well on its way towards a positive end.

On the other hand, if a suitable pursuit could not be found or local opportunities could not be found to fulfil the need, further effort will be required to possibly create such an opportunity.

It may be possible that by collecting information about the types of opportunities suitable to engage those "Lost" individuals, by grouping information from a large enough number of individuals, patterns of regional strengths may emerge. These patterns could be offered to local government, employers and potential investors who may be able to make such opportunities a reality for mutual benefit.

Such information may already exist in the databases of employment agencies and job centres for those jobless individuals from the mainstream.

An all inclusive approach that brings together all those requiring opportunities to contribute to society for mutual benefit, may present a more powerful and compelling scenario to employers and investors in an ever more competitive world.

The ability to present a regional capacity of creative, manual and intellectual manpower resources from the mainstream as well as from those marginalised elements in society will undoubtedly improve the potential for those individuals and for their regions.

The only danger in this process is the risk of protracted periods that turn off individuals and potential employers away from the process. Any sense of disillusion in the process will kill the process and alienate the marginalised beyond the point of recovery. Therefore, such a position must be avoided at all costs.

A possible means of holding the interest of all individuals, who have built up an expectation, is to keep them active. This may be by involving them in either:
- charitable community fun schemes or
- a few specialist government supported and
      funded commercial or industrial non-profit
      making but self-financing enterprises
until such time as mainstream employment positions could be found in the wider community.

It would be important to remove any potential stigma that may be associated with such schemes or non-profit making enterprises in the eyes of both the participants and the general public by ensuring they are labelled and are given a commercial image and business brand.

Outwardly, such enterprises or schemes should appear and interact as any other mainstream business. However, internally, they need to have flexible structures that can be moulded to suite their main purpose of rehabilitation.

Such an approach could be additionally valuable as training grounds towards self-restraint under close supervision and with professional guidance.

As well as engaging the "Lost" youths and turning them away from the "mindless and destructive" behaviours, the benefits of such an approach are so wide and varied that it cannot be dismissed.

It could be perceived that any financial or human resource costs associated with such an approach would be more than recovered by:
- the lower cost of the aftermath of crime
- the evolving productive output from those previously excluded
- the opportunity to include other marginalised non-productive members of society in this process
- the opportunity to provide behavioural and vocational training under controlled safe conditions
- the ability to offer the wider community, a valuable pool of resources that would have been potentially wasted
- the reduced cost to government and society of funding unemployment support

…. and the list goes on ….

INTERNATIONAL RELATIONS

On the simplest level, International Relations are about communications and interactions between nation groups of humans and how they collectively view each other and subsequently judge each others' collective actions.

However, International Relations are far more complex. Like all human relations, international or otherwise, they are affected by a variety of factors including:
- the personality traits of the individuals participating in the interactions, appearance, charisma, linguistic and communication skills, intellectual ability ...etc
- the history of previous interactions between interacting parties
- self-interests taking the form of hidden agendas
- allegiances and power pacts with other parties that affect the perceived balance of power
- the negotiating skills and resources employed by one party compared to the others.
- the long-term generational memory imprint of historic conflicts between interacting nation groups.
- the contribution or benefit one party brings to the relationship compared to others.
.... etc

International Relations like all human individual relationships can be positive or negative, mutually constructive or destructive, co-operative or conflict-ridden, amicable or resentful ... etc

We can view the network of International Relations across all the nations on this earth as a system that is man-made with all its inputs and outputs being those listed above and more.

As with any other system, there has to be an acceptable region of balance that the system can operate within and that can maintain a balance far away enough from influences that push the boundaries to such a degree that they create a Pendulum effect.

The obvious expectation for the average individual is for such a system of International Relations to bring benefit to themselves and the group or nation they consider themselves to belong to.

Such an expectation automatically pits one nation group against another whenever conflicts of interests arise.

Without moderating influences, International Relations can be very fragile and can easily breakdown.

It is the skill of international diplomacy to apply such moderating influences and maintain channels of communication and potential co-operation between nation groups.

The difficulty faced in International Relationships throughout human history and to a large degree at the start of the 21st century is that various nation groups do not necessarily recognise the importance of a region of balance in these relationships, nor do they consider the prevailing region of balance to represent their interests sufficiently.

The nature of constantly changing national identity by amalgamations of sub-groups or the division of larger national regions into smaller sub-groups, puts pressure on such a system to find new regions of balance to accommodate the altered nation groups.

Also, a fast changing world of international commerce and instant communications, alongside technological advances that alter the world view of natural and human resource capacities and patterns around the world, provides for a constantly changing picture of who and where various self-interests lie with.

The "United Nations" organisation was effectively created as a forum to bring representations of all the various national interests together in a melting pot to then reach amicable or at least common decisions that should avoid bipartisan conflicts.

The difficulty encountered with the United Nations is that its structure was created at a particular time when a certain pattern of power bases prevailed around the world. However, patterns of power bases are constantly changing.

Recent changes that allowed for small changes in the panel of the United Nations Security council and other changes made to make debating and decision making processes more inclusive and more representative of the various nation groups around the world is a recognition of our changing world.

For the United Nations Organisation to continue to provide and continue to be seen to provide a forum for diplomacy and moderating arbitration between nation groups, it will need to continue to evolve and change to become even more inclusive and more equally representative of the interests of all national groups in the decision making processes as well as the debates.

In the mean time, many nation groups who have felt that the United Nations did not sufficiently allow for their interests to be represented, have circumvented International Forums and acted on pure self-interest in an almost rebellious manner. Such nation states have often been referred to as "Rogue States".

Those Rogue states have responded to other nation states in a similar manner to that exhibited by rebellious violent youths in their own small community.

It may be possible to correlate the reasons and the best responses to have between such Rogue States in the World Community and the Rebellious Violent Youths in the Local Community.

Just like most rebellious violent youths who are not 'Undeterred' criminals, Rogue States are likely to be responding to what they perceive are oppressive conditions or a situation that marginalises them and their interests and does not value their contribution.

Also, just like marginalised individuals in a community, most actually want to belong to the community and want the community to value them. The problem is neither side can work out or is prepared to take the steps necessary to achieve that appropriately and with minimal conflict.

In the main Rogue States can be rehabilitated just like individuals can with provision of reasonable understanding from their world community and readiness to interact and communicate to find ways that valued contributions can be made in both directions for mutual benefit.

Good international relations and diplomacy should be capable of bringing all national groups into the fold and minimise the damage that can be caused by unrestrained actions leading to wars that can easily flare up and become hot beds for further larger conflicts. Something that is surely not in the interest of the majority of the world's population.

Leaders of nations and states set the tone for many international relationships and interactions that can either make or break negotiations and diplomacy.

That is why the choices that nation groups make in selecting their leaders can have enormous influence on the wider international community.

None-the-less, an inclusive approach for all leaders of nation groups, no matter what their perceived position may be, is crucial. World leaders need to be individuals who are capable of putting personalities and appearances aside and come together regularly and collectively to breakdown barriers and open channels for diplomacy and conciliation.

In our evolving world community, with travel and communications becoming easier and quicker, there is little excuse for nation leaders to allow exclusion or permit small inevitable conflicts of interests to fester over periods of time and develop into larger conflicts. This is likely to be the first step to arrive at and maintain a better balanced and more harmonious world society.

Promoting and operating international relations on the basis of Power Dominance and on the basis of Adversarial Face-offs is likely to conclude with international strategies that lead to situations like the two world wars and the East-West cold war of the 20th century, the Middle-East Israel-Arab face-offs and the Gulf wars amongst others.

But what about internal conflicts within a nation state and civil war?
What should the international community do if anything?
A difficult question with ambiguous conclusions!

No doubt that we cannot stand-by and watch injustices being perpetrated by one group against another even within a nation state. It is our duty to at least put a stop to injustice. How that can be achieved must depend on the parties involved, the personalities and the history.

However, one thing is certain, whatever the personalities or the history, the international community must intervene as a moderator and a conciliator with an objective to immediately halt injustices perpetrated and immediately follow up with supervised process of negotiations and diplomacy.

To arrive at an immediate halt of injustices, the international community has to be united vocally and actively to put aside individual national interests and place pressures of all kinds and of significant magnitudes on the warring parties or the party perpetrating the injustice, to unconditionally stop their actions.

However, any action the international community applies to halt any injustices must be made without resort to violence. Else, the international community itself could potentially become the perpetrator of injustice, something that must be avoided at all costs, as this nullifies any efforts to redress any imbalance that already exists and becomes itself a cause of imbalance.

There are multitudes of avenues open to the international community to put pressure on warring parties, from simple diplomacy to enticements with rewards to threats of isolation and embargoes there will be many non-violent options open for negotiations.

The halting of injustices will be a first step that paves the way for opportunities to move to resolve the conflict peacefully.

BALANCE IN DAILY LIFE

Even if we do not recognise it, whether busy or quiet, happy or sad, the lives of all individuals consist of regular repeating patterns of activities and a varying proportion of irregular activity.

Routines are those regular activities that we carry out in a similar manner at regular time intervals. They bring some form of order into our lives.

Our daily routines are the backbone of all our activity. Very few of us exist from day to day without having some regular routines that we follow even if they are minimalist.

Those routines are built around the prevailing requirements of our daily lives. From the road sweeper to the prime-minister to the president, we all have basic bodily function routines.

Some basic routines are common and are typically learnt, encouraged and practised during childhood. Their objectives are to establish a regular process of maintenance of our physical bodies, such as sleeping, eating, washing hands, bathing, grooming, brushing teeth, medical and dental check ups, cleaning and upkeep of habitable environment …etc.

Some other basic maintenance routines are more personal and represent the character of the individual. Their objectives are to promote a clearer state of mind or to improve a personal projection or status in society.

Routines such as reading, keeping up with news events, shopping, attending social group events ...etc.

Other non-basic routines that we develop as individuals depend much on our life style, work demands and social positions. These routines are very particular and specific to each individual with mixes that also exhibit our character and what image we are trying to project.

In addition, we all follow ambitious pursuits of particular life objectives, be that an interest or hobby, a job promotion or a financial enterprise, a position or status, a personal relationship or a particular pleasure or even at a basic level, just our needs for essential survival, like ensuring, food, shelter and warmth.

Such life pursuits and the mixes of choices we make or those imposed upon us by circumstances, often dictate the mix of routines we need to develop to sustain that mix.

More importantly, routines are learnt activities that we become very adept at, requiring less and less concentration and attention as we become better practiced at them.

Essentially, by turning our regularly required activities into mundane routines, we reduce the amount of energy we need to dedicate towards their maintenance, leaving more time and energy to dedicate to dealing with those events that do not occur regularly or those that are not expected.

In a busy modern life the demands of our life styles and personal pursuits are so many and varied. The use of diaries, personal organisers, time-management techniques and the like, are our attempts to bring some form of order and routine to events that are not typically routine so we are more able to handle them.

Even if we are not consciously aware, by creating and following life routines, we are establishing a systematic structure with anticipated balances in activities that meet our perceived needs at all levels.

If we lose sight of that balance, when certain demands on our lives become more significant than they should be, which is inevitable by the nature of the variability of events, we are unable to recognise the imbalance created so that we can address it appropriately.

In such situations, the individual experiences heightened anxiety and stress, that has knock on effects in relation to their ability to deal with the imbalance and in relation to their physical health and wellbeing.

At such junctures, many find themselves at a loss about what to do. Confusion sets in. Uncertainty, and more stress follow.

Within groups of humanity where the family unit is strong and the extended family group is at hand to help and assist, individuals confide in those members of the family or extended family they have learnt to trust. They do that in the knowledge that the collective family interest lies in offering them genuine help and advice that will relieve their stress and assist them in resolving the imbalance they are experiencing in their life.

In some modern societies where the family unit has broken down and the extended family is almost non-existent, some rely on friends that they feel they can trust, but many seek professional councillors and psychotherapists to fulfil the gap and provide the advice needed.

Professional advice may provide some clarity and direction that were clouded or missing about how to deal with a particular life imbalance, but the follow-through to actual real improvement in the individual's life relies on the individual themselves.

When friendships are genuine and close, help is at hand, but for many, true friendships are difficult to come by, and in the absence of helpful friends and close family units to assist, modern life can be extremely difficult.

We necessarily demand more and more of governmental and local authorities and charitable organisations to provide resources to fill the other missing gap in actual assistance, by requesting home-help, dialling support phone lines, demanding respite care, receiving financial income support ....etc.
This is a symptom of the breakdown in the traditional support systems provided by the family unit and the extended family structure.

Having recognised the need to offer advice and assistance to many individuals who need them by whatever means are available to them, many more individuals are often able to readjust the imbalances in their lives without further help.

The best way to deal with most imbalances in our lives is by dealing with them ourselves. When we do that successfully, it gives us confidence and builds into us greater strength to handle more of life's difficulties. As the saying goes, "What does not kill you, can make you stronger".

So, how can we attempt to resolve our own life style imbalances ourselves?

Most individuals have reserves of knowledge, abilities and resources within themselves that they are not always aware of. For those individuals, there is a good chance they can resolve their own imbalance. But there will always be some individuals who will need advice and assistance and they should seek it where they can suitably find it.

It is probably true to say that the best way to remove an imbalance is not to have it in the first place. As another saying goes "prevention is better than cure".

By recognising our own life as a system of routines, we can consciously consider the best mix of routines for ourselves that would maintain an acceptable balance. There is only one criterion that must be fulfilled which is to ensure the basic routines for maintaining our healthy physical existence are carried out. These basic routines may vary from one individual to another depending on their prevailing state of health.

The saying that goes "a healthy mind is in a healthy body" is somewhat unfair to some individuals with some health issues but who have very capable minds. None-the-less, the saying emphasises the importance of maintaining our daily routines to look after our health as a pre-requisite to other activity.

All other demands on our life's routines are life style choices and we should be able to modify and change them if appropriate and necessary. Easier said than done for many.

On many occasions, those other life-style choices we make can in fact have a detrimental effect on our health. Such choices should not be made hastily. Moreover, we should be constantly questioning ourselves about our motives in pursuing damaging life-style choices and whether the benefits we perceive to get from them are genuine and worthwhile.

A case in point are addictive behaviours that start off in what initially appears to be fun life-style choices but ends up being very destructive, smoking, regular excessive alcoholic consumption, gambling, substance abuse …etc.

This process of questioning ourselves and making conscious decisions about our life-style choices in the light of their perceived outcomes is at the heart of resolving any imbalances in our daily life routines.

When we are unaware, unable, or unwilling to put ourselves through this conscious process, we feel trapped in the cycle of daily events, being part of a rat race and having a feeling that we lost control over our lives.

Step back, reflect, identify those routines, make a conscious choice about the mix of routines to follow and set personal expectations that are achievable and sustainable. Follow-through by practising that mix of routines, allowing for a little realistic flexibility.

Contentment is probably the goal of what many refer to, unknowingly, as the "quality of life". Not as some would perceive it to be through material gain or gadgets acquired ...etc.

Shopping for goodies on the local high-street, for those fortunate enough to afford it, may provide short term therapy for some, a kind of emotional release during the shopping process and a distraction from daily stresses by enjoying the purchases for a little while afterwards.

But that does not address the source of the stresses we feel, and the stresses soon return.

The shopping process can become a dangerous addiction to some. Just like substance abuse, the relief is short lived and the individual's psyche demands that more relief is found, creating a cycle of addiction that must be recognised and must be dealt with as such.

As many would recognise nowadays, money does not buy happiness. They say it can make the bitter pill easier to swallow! But a better way would be to find that cure that is so elusive to many.... An appropriate balance and a contentment built on reasonable expectations.

That is not to say that contentment should mean a lack of ambition. But a driving ambition with reasonable expectations will minimise disappointment and help maintain sensible contentment.

In fact, by our nature, without ambition, many individuals would find life very dreary. This in itself can be a source of stress and discontent in an individual's life.

Again, it is the appropriate balance between ambition and expectations that will help us achieve the contentment we need.

DIET & EXERCISE

As many may already recognise, human physiology is effectively a system of inputs and outputs.

We consume foods and drinks and breath air as inputs so that our bodies can process those inputs to release energies and nutrients that allow our bodies to function, grow and heal. Our bodies expend outward energy, radiate thermal energy and expel waste as outputs.

The difference in energy and nutrients between the inputs we consume and the outputs we expend, are the energy and nutrients either used up inside our bodies to function, do work, grow and heal or are stored away in temporary buffers that our bodies are naturally and very cleverly designed to create.

Our bodies store much of the excess energy and nutrients when those inputs are plentiful, so that the body can use those stored buffers at times when there is a shortage of energy and nutrients intake. Historically, that refers to seasonal times of plenty followed by seasonal shortages of food and nutrients.

The buffer stores that our bodies create are mainly in the form of fat reserves that represent excess energy intake not yet needed.

For those mathematically inclined, a simple equation for a system of inputs and outputs:
Differential = Input - Output
  -ve Differential = Fat Reserve Burnt = Lose Weight
  +ve Differential = Fat Stored = Gain Weight

So what about diets and dieting?
All those who want or need to lose weight.....

Well..... let us consider that there are two categories of
dieters, the habitual dieters who follow a quick on-off
dieting regime, and the serious all-or-nothing one off
dieters.

Dieting is a traumatic process that is psychologically
difficult, but more so it is physically difficult and
potentially damaging.

Habitual on-off dieters appear to follow in the main
moderate dieting regimes that act almost as tweaking
controls over an average body weight that they maintain
over long periods of time.

This begs the question of why do habitual dieters feel a
need to make themselves suffer the trauma of even
moderate dieting regimes when all they are doing is
maintain a fairly steady state?

A better approach for those habitual dieters may be to
just consider normal eating habits with all the foods they
normally would eat and enjoy, but just a small reduction
in quantity in all their meals. This sensible intake of food
combined with moderate exercise to maintain a balance
of inputs and outputs should be more than sufficient to
maintain a steady and healthy body weight.

To describe a hypothetical example:
Scenario 1:
A habitual dieter that goes through a period, say over the
Christmas holidays where they eat all the foods they like

and enjoy in excessive quantities and at the same time do little exercise. Just to put a figure on it, let us say three meals a day at an average of 500grams per meal, providing them with an excess energy and nutrient input that causes them to put on say 2Kgs over two weeks.

Holidays over, they do not like the bulge they developed over the holidays, so they feel stressed and pressured to lose weight. For the next month, they put themselves through the trauma of dieting with a lot of associated guilt and more stress.

Scenario 2:
The same individual in scenario 1, except that during the Christmas holidays, they also eat all the foods they like and enjoy, just slightly smaller portions, still three meals a day, but now at an average of only 450grams per meal. A sensible level of food intake together with some physical exercise in the form of a few walks enjoying the opportunity to de-stress in pleasant surroundings.

This is only a 10% reduction in the total amount of food they would have consumed in scenario 1. For every plateful they would have had, take away 1 slice in 10. Hardly noticeable.

Except that at the end of the two weeks holiday, there is no net gain in weight and no stress or guilt or need for any more trauma and stress from dieting for the following four weeks.

A simple balanced approach that gets rid of the yo-yo pattern of weight gain followed by weight loss then back again, up and down, on and on…. Let us call it the "anti-yoyo dieting and exercise regime" for habitual dieters.

We are all born with our own genetic code that is inherited from our ancestors and that determines our physical characteristics, our physiology and general appearance.

As much as we may wish to have a particular look or appearance, without radical surgery that may or may not give the expected results, we can only tweak at the edges of what nature and genetics have provided us with.

After all, it is not wrong, bad or necessarily visually off-putting to have a small well-positioned fat store that is normal and natural to have. In fact a small, well-positioned bulge may give some individual's a more attractive visual profile than without it. Just consider the slightly curvy looks of those ladies who are traditionally associated with being attractive throughout human history.

A healthy body is often better achieved by working with our bodies' natural systems than by attempting to force a particular appearance through either excessive exercise or through severe dieting regimes.

Let us remember that our human bodies are physical machines that very cleverly have a limited ability to self-heal and regenerate. Dieting and excessive physical exercise are extreme conditions that our bodies may be able to cope with for short periods of time. However, if excessive exercise or severe dieting are persistent, then our bodies are likely to suffer in the long term due to the imbalance these conditions impose.

Because genetics ensure a wide spectrum of physical and psychological abilities across a population, some individuals are more capable of accommodating more severe conditions than others. Some individuals are capable of training their bodies to respond to extreme exercise or dieting more than others. This allows them to adapt their bodily systems to different points of balance that they are able to sustain.

A careful gradual process of moving the points of balance can help some individuals achieve exceptional results. This is done very carefully and often very slowly, in a manner that maintains appropriate inputs and outputs all along the process to minimise any potential short or long term damage to their bodies. A case in point are body builders.

But most average individuals will only suffer if they make such attempts, especially if such attempts are made hastily and without proper planning to maintain appropriate nutritional and exercise balances.

Moderate exercise is necessary, healthy and sensible for most individuals. A balanced regime of exercise will vary slightly from one individual to another. However, excessive exercise can be as unhealthy as too little exercise to most individuals.

It is only the psychological manipulations in recent human history that have distorted our traditional view away from the slightly curvy female appearance. Left to our natural uninfluenced, un-manipulated instincts, the traditional curvy view would probably be the preferred choice again.

As for the all-or-nothing one-off dieters, theirs is likely to be the consequence of a seriously extreme overweight condition or a medical condition or both.

There may be genuinely good reasons for such all-or-nothing dieting. When that is the case, on balance, the trauma of dieting may be necessary and worthwhile.

Good reasons for dieting will always be on medical grounds including heart condition, cholesterol, seriously overweight, readiness for a theatre operation ...etc

All other reasons for dieting that are not on medical grounds may not be good enough reasons to justify the trauma of dieting.

None-the-less, personal freedom to make such choices dictates that each individual will also have to accept the consequences of their own actions, although it is recommended that no such decision about such dieting be made without medical approval and close medical supervision because of its potential dangers.

It important to remember that our bodies need a mixture of nutrients and energy sources to function correctly. These include small amounts of various kinds of fats, sugars, minerals, proteins, carbohydrates, vitamins, salts ...etc

Severe diets that cut out any particular range of food ingredients over a long period of time are likely to be damaging to our bodies, even if the dieter achieves the anticipated weight loss. Such a weight loss would be at the expense of long term health. Not necessarily a balance that is expected or acceptable.

What may be considered as "Healthy" foods because they are very low in fats, sugars, salts …etc may not provide a healthy meal on their own. Our bodies need that mix that includes those fats, sugars and salts that many individuals believe they should avoid. By not consuming the required amounts of those foods, those individuals could be jeopardising their health.

For individuals with particular medical conditions, the balance required in their diet will have to be as prescribed by their doctor.

However, for an average healthy individual, it is important not to cut out any foods from their diet, only make sure there is a sensible and appropriate balance in the various foods they eat.

Healthy individuals should be able to eat anything and everything that is suitable for human consumption but in moderate quantities. No need to cut out the sweets, chocolate, butter, salt, carbohydrates or anything else… just do not have too much of them.

In general, it is not what you eat that matters. It is how much you eat that will mostly make the difference.

Similarly, healthy individuals will naturally put their bodies through a moderate process of daily exercises, be that through our normal daily routines of walking, cleaning and doing productive work, or through a more planned moderate exercise routines in the gym.

Always remember, too much exercise can be as bad, damaging and unhealthy as too little exercise.

A correct balance of food intake and exercise are necessary for the healthy long-term operation of our human body.

Too much restriction on food intake will weaken our bodies. While unrestricted food intake will burden our bodies with imbalances that strain our bodily systems.

Too much exercise will wear our bodies out gradually and unsustainably. While too little exercise will cause lethargy and result in a greater tendency to not burn up or use the energy and nutrients that we eat, subsequently causing our bodies to build up unnecessary fat reserves that will slow us down further. Thus creating a state of bodily imbalance that reduces our productive potential.

OBESITY

There is a recent tendency to blame diet and concentrate on food intake as a cause of weight gain.

The much maligned fatty foods, salty foods, sugary foods ...etc are often marked up as causes of modern day obesity.

As an example, let us look more carefully at the changes that have happened in recent time in western European countries and North America.

A greater access to fast food outlets is undeniable. However, is that alone enough to cause obesity amongst a population?

Also, a greater availability of high energy sugary foods is undeniable. Again, is that a sufficient cause for an obese population?

Let us recall, as described in an earlier chapter, that both diet and exercise are inextricable components of an energy balance equation.

The greater access to an increasing range of certain foods over others, alongside marketing and pricing strategies by the suppliers of such products will entice the majority of consumers to purchase and eat such foods.

We all need food as an energy source and there is certainly nothing wrong with making energy rich foods more accessible to more people. In fact, in a world where poverty and famine still prevails, this may be desirable!

Obesity is an obvious symptom of an imbalance.

As with other imbalances, the most effective solutions are those that identify the causes of the imbalances and then target appropriate actions at either removing the causes of the imbalance or minimising their impact.

So, what are the causes of the imbalance that leads to obesity?

Some may suggest that the availability of fast food outlets or the number of sugary or fatty foods on offer are the cause of the problem. But let us remember that all foods are healthy, and the availability of food cannot be a bad thing.

Problems typically arise when balance is lost.
For an individual to become obese, they must have consumed foods far in excess of their daily needs for energy that is required to function, do work, heal and grow over a long period of time.

An excessive consumption of high energy, high fat foods alongside minimal or steady bodily energy requirement over a long period will undoubtedly push an individual towards obesity.

To identify the causes of obesity, we need to consider the factors that contribute to excessive consumption of energy compared with daily energy needs.

Let us differentiate between weight gain and obesity.

Weight gain is a natural process that is part of our human physiology. It is typically balanced by the equally natural process of weight loss. The pattern of gains and losses may follow a natural seasonal, monthly or individual profile that may be particular to an individual and that maintains a typical average weight.

On the other hand, Obesity is a forced state of imbalance where high levels of weight gain are maintained over long periods that are not part of a natural process of seasonal or periodic gain-loss profile.

Modern day life is increasingly demanding that individuals spend more time being focused on tasks that require less and less physical and mental energy to perform than was the case when people had to forage or hunt for their food and their survival.

We are generally better clothed and housed, have an increasingly expanding range of energy saving devices, with access to energy resources increasingly easier and more accessible.

While our physiology still requires a minimum intake of food, our psychology is naturally inclined to consume food in periods of plenty so that we can cope with periods of drought.

In addition, our psychology is also naturally inclined to consume a greater amount of food, if it is available, when there are increased physical or mental demands placed on our bodies.

Even though the physical demands of modern day life may not be high, the mental demands in the form of stress and tension are recognised as elevated.

Our psychology converts that energy demand from stress and tension into a desire to consume food if it is available. Many people would recognise that in the phrase "comfort eating".

The availability of high fat and high energy foods like sugary sweets and chocolate has prevailed for the last few centuries of human history, whereas, the increasing levels of obesity in populations has only become prevalent in the last few decades.

What has changed in these last few decades that contributed towards the tendency towards obesity?

It is unlikely to be the foods, whether fatty, sugary, deliciously chocolatey or otherwise!

However, it is apparent that our energy saving modern life styles have reduced the expenditure of bodily physical energy where powered vehicles have reduced walking energy and the energy needed to compensate for heat losses in cold surrounding environments.

As well as our need to consume food for survival, our physiology is designed to make us appreciate and enjoy the process of eating and tasting foods. We also enjoy heightened levels of energy that make us feel more able to do more of the things we enjoy doing.

Eating for pleasure, so long as it does not create unsustainable imbalance, is a reasonable and a worthwhile activity that improves our psychological state and makes us better able to deal with the events of daily life.

With all that in mind, focusing our attention either solely or even primarily on removing a few selected foods from an individual's diet is not seeing the whole picture and not tackling the true causes of obesity.

For example, to deprive children of sweets and chocolate on grounds that they may rot their teeth or that they may contribute to obesity is very short sighted!

Children enjoy sweets and chocolates, that are good healthy foods in moderate quantities, just like all adults do. To deprive any individual of these foods is unreasonable. More over, children need high energy food sources for their faster growth and their energetic activities. Sweet and chocolates are ideal sources.

To be concerned about rotting teeth is reasonable. However, the solution to preventing tooth decay is not to stop eating sweets and chocolates, but is in better oral cleanliness and hygiene. The solution is to make sure children clean their teeth and wash their mouths more frequently, even several times a day if necessary.

To be concerned about obesity is reasonable. However, the solution to preventing obesity is not to stop eating the occasional fast food meal or to stop eating sweets and chocolate, but is in having a balanced range of meals and ensuring an equal energy expenditure. The solution is to make sure the children use up sufficient energy in physical and mental exercises that balance out any excess energy from their food energy intake.

All foods are healthy in appropriate quantities. It is important to remove the stigma attached to certain foods and particular diets. What matters is balance, as always.

To that end, preventing obesity must be viewed from a perspective of:
1- reasonable self-restraint in not eating to excess
2- choosing a full range of foods in a balanced manner
3- expending excess energy intake through reasonable and balanced physical and mental exercises, through sports, games, projects, nature trails …etc

A balanced approach to food and meals and to physical and mental exercises should be enjoyable and productive. It is in the nature of a balanced approach to be natural, acceptable and reasonable. With a little insight and understanding, this should make it easier to implement.

The genetics of the individual is a further complicating factor in this balancing equation, in that the genetics dictate the tendency of a human body to store fat reserves. The tendency of our bodies to burn up the energy that we consume in the form of food is affected by the body metabolism as well as the physical activity we do.

The body metabolism represents the amount of work and energy the body uses in maintaining its normal internal functions. This will vary from one person to another.

LADIES AND THEIR FIGURES

This chapter is for you ladies.....

What is it about thin figures that makes some believe they are attractive?

As referred to in the previous chapter, traditionally, it is the slightly curvy, voluptuous appearance that is naturally seen to be attractive in the human female form.

For good reasons, the natural instinct of the human male in the majority is to be attracted to women with a little fat reserve but not too much. Such a curvy appearance suggests the woman is healthy and is traditionally capable of drawing on that reserve store in times of hardship.

Also, whether still correctly interpreted in the modern society of the early 21st century or not, the slightly larger female with the slightly larger bosom and the slightly curvy bottom is traditionally and naturally associated more with improved chances of childbearing and of child rearing capacity.

That is likely to make the human male in general, more attracted to a large curvy female than a very slim, flat featured female. Although, they say "Love is Blind"!

This is evident in the continuing tendency to portray women with a large bosom as attractive. In fact it is still a very highly sought after attribute to seek, even by females looking for breast augmentation because they believe it makes them more attractive.

So what is it with the waistband, the hips and the buttocks that has changed in recent times to make females believe they are more attractive if they were small or flat?

Could it be a misconception brought on by the media portraying those young female models wearing the designer clothes on the catwalk?

It is possible that the need of clothes designers to employ individuals who are almost featureless to present their clothes has distorted the expectations of women.

Women in general in recent times seem to aspire to become display manikins for those designer clothes.

Catwalk models are selected with the main objective of being good at displaying the clothes they are given without drawing attention to themselves and without detracting away from the clothes they are trying to sell.

Surely, that is not what women want! Or it is?

No matter what can be concluded from this observation, there is no doubt that the increasingly more extreme selection of increasingly slimmer models for the catwalk is drawing louder objections from health professionals and from the general public.

Employing Size-Zero models is ethically and morally questionable. It serves to reinforce the view expressed above that catwalk model are merely featureless walking display manikins for the clothes that they are given to present.

There is no doubt that the pressure experienced by those young female models distorts the balance in their lives to such an extent that it seriously jeopardises their health.

That is why there are many growing voices who are calling for a ban on the use of size-zero models on the catwalks.

Maybe this will offer some re-balancing influence to the distorted view that slim and featureless waistband, hips and buttocks are actually desirable.

Size-zero is recognised as a seriously negative image for other young impressionable females to be presented with as an example to aspire to. It places unrealistic and undesirable pressures on young women who either

- fail to achieve their aspiration of size-zero, resulting in stress and very often self-harm through Bulimia and through physical punishment of their uncooperative body

- or those who succeed in reaching size-zero at a great cost to their health and long-term wellbeing.

We are all individuals and we come in all shapes and sizes. If we did not and we were all the same, life would be very dreary.

In addition, because of the diversity in individual characters, what appeals to one person may not appeal to another. This is part and parcel of nature's variety.

Despite all our differences, most of us have common needs, similar ambitions and an instinctive desire to find our soul-mate, our knight-in-shining-armour, our tall-dark-stranger, our prince or princess, our partner-for-life, that someone who understands us, who is prepared to stand by us and share our joy as well as our sadness, our desires and our fears, so that together we can make life's trials more meaningful and it's tribulations more tolerable.

There is likely to be that someone out there for every one of us that will bring the added balance to our lives. It is often a question of a chance encounter and a mutual recognition. When you find them, they will not care much whether you are thin or fat, slight in build or large in frame, short or tall, black or white, blond or dark hair. It is the person inside that will shine and bring you together.

So, if you haven't found that special person, don't give up, they may be still out there.....

And if you are with your special someone, work at that relationship. It takes a mutual desire to keep the flame burning. Find the balance between the needs and desires of both of you. It is a changeable balance that needs constant effort and adjustment.... Keep the balance and you will always be attractive to each other, no matter what your figure is like.

CONSERVATION & PRESERVATION

To recall that the world around us is constantly and naturally changing gives us cause to permit ourselves to accept that change is acceptable.

Someone once said, "the only certain thing in life is change"!

So why do we so often feel inclined to insist on and expect that conservation and preservation should be an objective and a pursuit?

Individuals by nature expect routines, as described in an earlier chapter. Routines are built around repeating activities that rely on expectations of repeating situations.

Normally that is acceptable for daily routines short-term patterns of repeating situations. Our natural ability to adapt allows us to cope with minor variations and changes over a period of time that makes the individual small step changes almost unnoticeable.

It is possible that at times, this normally acceptable expectation of a short-term steady state set of routines, is extended to medium and long-term events.

When that happens, alongside the observable natural changes in situations, it engenders a desire within those individuals to attempt and preserve or conserve what previously existed but is no longer appropriate or applicable.

No doubt there is a role for some conservation and preservation amongst very few objects or situations that can be used for study, demonstration or commercial value.

But in the majority of situations where some individuals have a tendency to try and preserve or conserve, their efforts are probably misdirected and even wasteful, as there is often little benefit in the conservation or the preservation except to satisfy a personal desire.

Take the attempts at rescuing animal or plant species that are on the verge of extinction, not by the careless actions of mankind, but by the normal natural process of selection and survival of the fittest. For such species, nature has made its decision and we should respect it.

Equally, take some old buildings that may be from a particularly interesting historic era, but they are no longer in regular use and are no longer fit for purpose. In such circumstances, preventing redevelopment or even disposal of such structures because they may be "historic" is not always appropriate.

A balanced approach means that it is necessary to consider each case on its merits by recognising the impacts of the various inputs and outputs related to the system of balance relevant to that case.

FREEDOM, LIBERALISM &
RESPONSIBILITY

In the land of the free, freedom is highly prized.

But what freedom?
It is implicit in many people's understanding of freedom
that it is not unrestricted or unlimited.

It seems almost a contradiction in terms to recognise
that we cannot be free to exercise unrestrained freedom
to do whatever we may desire.

That is because freedom comes at a price. If we act freely
and without any reference to prevailing situations,
circumstances and with disregard to others and to the
world around us, then we risk that our actions may be at
odds with the balances needed for immediate and future
sustainability.

By virtue of our existence in the world around us,
whether we like it or not, we are part of the earth
envelope system and our actions are, in effect, direct
inputs into that system.

In return, we are directly influenced and affected by the
earth envelope system. That includes, amongst others,
nature, the environment, human society, our community
and our family and friends.

So what does it really mean to be free?

It may be clear to most of us that we have to temper and
moderate our actions and reactions in our everyday lives

to allow us to interact positively and productively with other individuals and with the world around us.

As individuals, we have frustrations and emotions that can easily well-up inside of us like a volcano that is about to erupt, and on occasion, some of us are guilty of letting such emotions erupt and disrupt and destroy.

Relationships are in essence pathways and roadways for communicating ideas, understanding, emotions and feelings. But by their nature, these relationship pathways are very fragile and can be easily damaged.

The collection of relationships that we accumulate during our lifetime is effectively a network of those pathways that together act as a system in their own right and with ourselves at the centre of our network.

Damage caused by any imbalance to one part of this relationships network can easily have impact elsewhere in our network system. We often encounter this kind of effect when a damaged relationship between two family members spills over to other relationships within the family.

That is why it is in our own interest as individuals to look after all of our relationship pathways.

It is often said that we are all born free. That may be true at the time of our birth, where our relationships are limited to a mutual physical and psychological need between mother and baby.

However, as soon as we start to develop any kind of relationship with others or start to recognise our impact on our environment and our surroundings, our personal freedom starts to be curtailed.

Exercising our personal freedom without attention to our relationships is ultimately counterproductive.

Too much freedom can be seen as anarchy. An "anything goes" mentality is questionably off-balance by definition. While too much protection from personal freedoms can also be seen as repressive and oppressive.

The balance has to be between personal freedoms and protecting the individual and the public interest. Such a fine balance is very difficult to strike at times, especially with a constantly changing system of balances and re-balances as relationship networks are by their nature.

Where do the limits to our personal freedoms lie so that we do not cause any inadvertent damage to our relationships and to our world?

The answer to that question can only be generalised, because the details depend on the nature of the relationship, the strength of the relationship, the impact of any damage on other relationships and the prevailing circumstances associated with that relationship.

Our freedom is valuable and we want to exercise it to the maximum limit we can without causing damage. So, in essence, that has to be the extent of our personal freedom, any action that causes any damage or harm to people, property or the environment should be considered as outside the limits of our personal freedom.

The limits to our personal freedoms should also be curtailed to prevent any gradual degeneration in our ability to recognise regions of balance and our ability to pass on our stable balanced systems to future generations of humanity.

Equally, we could view liberalism as a politicised extension of personal freedoms.

A liberal attitude to acceptable behaviour is that where tolerance of diversity is synonymous with the freedom to exist and to practice, while at the same time exercising a social conscious in maintaining a set of balances that sustain our society and our environment.

Liberalism should be the ambition of a society that
- recognises balances, personal, social and environmental
- Applies practical measures to engender a sense of ownership and responsibility to individual and collective actions
- Sets clear boundaries for the essential regions of balance needed for future sustainability.
- Allows the freedom to act as seen fit
- Gauges the quality of actions by their ability to sustain the regions of balance
- Then, applies restorative and retribution justice impartially and severely to ensure sustainability of balances for the future.

After all, freedom and ownership of our own actions whether individually or collectively go hand-in-hand with responsibility.

Responsibility is

- the need to approach all of our actions responsibly in the way we assess their impact and in the manner that we apply them.

- equally, the readiness for accountability, to accept and shoulder all the consequences of our actions to the full. Including the full severity of an impartial and consistent justice system.

EDUCATION

When it is said that "We are all born equal", this is a powerful statement of expectations.

The understanding of what these expectations may represent can be easily manipulated, misconstrued and misdirected.

"Equality" is often referred to in the context of equality of possessions, equality in power, equality in position, equality in pay ..... etc.

Such "equality" is not conducive to balance and true equality. After all, how is it equal to be offered equal pay to two work colleagues who are not equally productive or who do not have equal skill or experience.

How is it equal for two individuals to expect equal power and authority over a decision when only one of the individuals carries the responsibility for that decision and is expected to accept and fully shoulder the consequences of any such decision?

Therefore, "equality" can only truly be "Equality of Opportunity" and "Equality of Rights to Access Opportunities". It is then up to the individual to make the best of their opportunities.

There cannot be a blanket "Equality of Rights". That is because "Rights" go hand-in-hand with "Responsibility" as previously described.

So, how do we provide for "Equality of Opportunity"?

The starting point in all our attempts towards equality of opportunity must be in education.

An education system that offers our young, up-and-coming individuals with knowledge, skills, experience and confidence to face situations, be productive and earn the psychological and material wealth that they deserve in relation to their abilities, their energy and their determination.

It is also an education system that delivers a balance view of our world and helps all members of our human society to recognise commonly accepted regions of balance, while at the same time encourage ambition and industry and engender ownership, responsibility and accountability.

To deliver such an effective education, we need inspired and experienced educators to change mindsets, counter preconceived ideas and reverse degenerative social and behavioural attitudes.

An effective education system empowers educators to face adverse reactions from damaged individuals and from damaging behaviour, so they can offer guidance towards clear cut boundaries and offer leadership by example.

The learning process always starts with copying. That is why the early years in the lives of our young individuals are so influential.

The role of the family, parents and teachers in presenting a moderate, balanced and productive example for the young to copy and aspire to can put the youngsters on a faster track towards self-improvement and development towards becoming valuable and valued members of society.

However, education is not the only delivery channel for balance and a balance view of the world in our human societies. It is only the starting point.

DELIVERY SYSTEMS

As previously described, the learning process includes learning by example. Learning "What To Do" as much as learning "What Not To Do"!

Leadership by example is a great educator. Whether parents, religious leaders, politicians, governments or just trusted friends, leading by example can show us one way or another!

To deliver a balance view to the general public, like any other message, the delivery channels are numerous and increasing with developing technologies.

However, in the main, there are obvious categorises for most of these channels:

- Educational Information
- Educational Establishments
- Government Legislation
- The Family
- Social Events and Projects
- Social Groups
- Media Reporting and News Channels
- Commercial Advertising
- Peer Pressure
- Religion
… etc

Naturally, educational information in the form of well written and presented books, leaflets, presentations and other worded and diagramatic material.

The role of educational establishments from Primary and Secondary Schools to Colleges to Universities. These establishments are hubs of knowledge and learning. A perfect channel to inform and guide those most able and most willing to learn and change.

Governments can play a vital role in delivering an urgency for needed change through legal legislative processes by changing laws, enforcing rules and regulations and by implementing deterrents and punitive measures.

The power of government legislation is immense and can be extremely effective. However, in using such powerful methods to deliver a message of required re-balance can itself be a cause of imbalance. The sudden powerful push of such legislation could initiate an undesirable swing of the pendulum. More often, a slow gradual process of change in the required direction can be more effective and longer lasting.

The family unit is the first nurturing environment that most children encounter as they conduct their existence into this world. That is not to deny the influence of other nurturing environments that do not revolve around a family unit.

None-the-less, for the majority, a strong well established family unit with a potential extended family support structure, provides a growing child with many examples to copy and aspire to. This continues until the child develops their ability to express their own character and individuality within the bounds of appropriate learnt boundaries that they have become familiar with during their earlier nurturing process.

A family unit that is guided by well balanced individuals can offer the love, care, education and example of responsible behaviour that a child needs in its early years.

For adult members of society and for older children, social groupings, social events and social projects become influential channels in delivering role models and examples of appropriate and acceptable balanced behaviours.

Whether it is a local celebration, a sports event, a hobbyist club or the like, these settings provide avenues for delivering an attitude of a life style balance. More importantly, they can act as powerful deterrents against unacceptable behaviours through the threats of social exclusion. For a social human animal, this can be a greater and longer lasting influence than law enforcement.

The roles of Media Reporting and News Channels whether newspapers, radio, television, cinema, recorded media, the internet or the like are well known. A well presented story with a targeted message, repeated over and over, can easily enter the consciousness of most individuals. Such stories have been used throughout human history as examples of cause and effect for future generations to take note of and learn from.

Before modern day media and the written word, news was delivered by story tellers and major influential stories were then passed on from one generation to the next. Some of those were simplified in the form of nursery rhymes that were mostly intended to inform, educate and warn the unwary child against potential dangers.

Modern news media still in essence does the same role. Historically, news stories that did not prove to be valuable and newsworthy were filtered out. Only those news stories that stood the test of time were carried forward and disseminated.

However, the pressure on 24/7 news media to fill space in written words, moving pictures and sound bites is increasingly creating an environment of trivia being labelled as news and for all reported news, trivial and serious, to be repeated endlessly.

There is a danger that such an approach to news delivery is itself out-of-balance to such an extent that it may either devalue the news message itself or desensitise those receiving it. The news media will then no longer provide valuable channels for delivering the message of balance that is needed.

By virtue of the ambitions of industry and commerce, Commercial Advertising has been grown in conjunction with very cleverly and carefully developed techniques that are often based on manipulating the psychology of those it is targeted at. It is a perfect channel for delivering the commercial messages that are intended.

A message of balance packaged in a similar manner as a commercial advertisement, and similarly and cleverly targeted to a particular audience can be delivered very effectively. The difficulty in this approach is that a commercial advertisement, although very costly to put together, will most likely recover the cost of advertising and more. Whereas a non-commercial message, packaged like a commercial advertisement, will be just as costly, but will not generate immediate financial return to cover costs. Even though the rewards of such a message of balance can be immense in the long term.

However the message of balance is delivered, it is the acceptance of that message by the key members of the targeted group that will eventually make the difference. That is the difference between the message becoming established instead of being heard and then lost in the mists of all the messages, news, information, and general entertainment trivia that wash over us incessantly.

A message that is heard and is acted upon, is internalised by the individuals acting on it. A powerful and long lasting effect that pervades further into a targeted group through peer pressure.

For a message to be accepted and internalised by an individual, it needs to reach them at a psychological level either by appealing to their ego or by praying on their fears or both.

Just like other delivery channels, a message of personal reward for expected and desired behaviour alongside a threat of severe godly retribution is a well established method for most religions to entice their followers towards particular behaviours.

At the core of modern day world-wide religions are messages of balance. Those religions that were not built on such a core message of balance have historically faded away. By their nature, only those world religions with a strong message of balance are likely to survive and spread amongst diverse world populations.

As such, those world-wide religions are very powerful and effective channels for spreading and reinforcing balances that are often much needed in a modern day uncertain world.

No matter what channels are used for delivering a message of balance, the effectiveness of the message depends on both the channel and on the nature of the message itself. A wrongly formulated message, however well intentioned, is potentially damaging.

Also, a well developed message of balance that is not well presented will fail to deliver the balance needed, no matter what channels are used.

Finally, in our modern day world, we are endlessly drowned by competing media, news, advertising, information, social and personal pressures.

Throughout human history, it is possible to recall examples of occasions when extremist, subversive or greedy individuals and groups have hijacked perfectly valuable and worthwhile delivery channels such as those described above for their own biased self-interests and have often caused undesirable imbalances.

Therefore, we must be very wary, as individuals, of those messages that are either ill thought through or that are maliciously and cleverly formulated to draw us to accept them when they may in fact cause either short term or long term damage to the balances we need.

Often, confusing messages can be as damaging as malicious ones. As an example, even though presented under the guise of harmless fun or being presented as coded speak, wrapping inappropriate acts in a shroud of goodness does not change their nature or their impact.

What confusing messages often intend to do, is to encourage others to relax their self-restraint and to act inappropriately without the associated feelings of guilt that assist in reinforcing self-restraint.

Using the label 'Bad' to suggest it means 'Good' is an obvious attempt at creating confusion. That is not to suggest individuals are so gullible to believe that bad is good. However, this undoubtedly works on a psychologically unconscious level that could relax perceptions to genuinely bad acts.

Not withstanding the confusing mix of messages we receive and should be wary of, at the same time we need to recognise those valuable worthy messages of balance and not throw them out with the bath water. In the massive mix of messages vying for our attention, this could be easier said than done.

REFLECTIONS

The sustainability of all life and the universe depends on the multitudes of balances that are historically and naturally self-regulating.

However, in the recent history on our Planet Earth, the influence of man-made events has become increasingly significant that the natural balances within the earth envelope system are being altered in ways that may affect the sustainability of life on Earth.

Also, the sustainability of our human societies will rely on our ability to work productively and to work together to improve our own existence and to improve our environment.

A growing world population, rapidly advancing technologies and faster, easier means of communications and travel are increasing the amount of human interactions exponentially. Consequently, the potential for reward as well as the potential for conflict and damage are also increasing exponentially.

Our need for sustainable balances has never been greater.

The issues of sustainable balances are in identifying the required regions of balance and then carefully and gradually edging towards them.

Avoiding pendulum effects and coping with constantly changing targets for regions of balance can make the process very demanding.

To simplify the complexity of maintaining sustainable balances, we should aim to create self-regulating systems with a minimum energy being required for manipulating modifying inputs.

We need to spread the message of balance through all available channels. But we need to be wary of ill thought or malicious messages.

Balance can only be achieved by having every able individual becoming a net contributor to the balance that is needed. The use of legislative and law enforcement channels are not often best for the majority of situations.

The message of balance needs to reach out to every individual at a psychological level.

For such a message to succeed, we have to avoid contradictions that can either dilute or alter the message. Avoid the situations of 'Do as I say Not as I do'.

As adult individuals, our psychology has evolved over the years since birth. It is the amalgam of all the influences we have experienced.

As young children, our points of reference are very few and are not well established. That is why the influences we experience in our earlier years can have a greater and longer lasting impact than our experiences from later years that are diluted and moderated by other factors.

For most children, the family unit, the school and their peers in their play groups are very influential in forming the individual's balance platform for the future.

Improving the strength of the family unit is engendered through:
- bringing a greater sense of duty from parents towards their children and their children's welfare.
- removing barriers that prevent parents from exercising appropriate authority to the parent-child relationship
- creating systems of retribution and greater deterrence against neglecting responsibilities
- ensuring parents present to their children a suitable role model and an example of appropriate balanced behaviour

Establishing a coherent, comprehensively planned and clear process of education through all available delivery channels to help children, parents and family units to re-establish, wherever necessary, balanced systems of interactions should allow all members of the family, adults as well as children, to grow and develop.

At the core of all behaviours and interactions emanating from every able individual is a system of internal checks and balances that we use within ourselves to exercise self-restraint. This is the most powerful force that affects all balances influenced by human activity.

Not to confuse ambition, industry and drive with self-restraint. It is perfectly normal and possible to be very ambitious, driven and industrious while at the same time exercise self-restraint against acts that create imbalance.

Personal choice and consumerism do not necessarily contradict with self-restraint, they are merely informed and moderated by it.

"The New Consumerism" should be responsibly guided consumerism that is subject to clear-cut boundaries.

Self-restraint acts to contain our human activity within appropriate boundaries that maintain regions of balance.

But what is an appropriate boundary for self-restraint and how do we make sure that all individuals know and adhere to those boundaries?

Some boundaries are easier to recognise and adhere to than others. Some boundaries need to be rigid, while others need to be flexible and adaptable. Such flexibility should be limited to allow them to remain within the regions of balance.

Historically those boundaries and the recognition of where they lie have grown and evolved within human societies over long periods of time and were passed through the generations.

In a situation where a state of balance has been lost, there is a need to have it re-established.

The best approach is probably to address the basics by recognising the primary inputs that influence these balances, moderate those inputs very gently and carefully to prevent pendulum effects, then allow the natural systems to gradually re-establish a recognisable balance that we can sustain over the long term.

Nature as evolved through the millennia has developed very resilient self-regulating systems that have a natural ability to re-adjust its balance. Any influence that our man-made events have on nature's systems may affect our habitable environment but may not be as significant in the greater natural system of balances.

It is important that we take appropriate measures to protect our environment and respect nature's systems. However, it is likely that nature will be resilient enough to the small influences that we may exert on it.

So long as we can act to prevent human actions that can alter balances seriously and significantly, our habitable environment is likely to remain sustainable. However, we will need to be adaptable enough to cope with natures own varying states of balance that it will throw at us and that are constantly and naturally changing.

This book is dedicated to
Susan

www.ingramcontent.com/pod-product-compliance
Lightning Source LLC
Chambersburg PA
CBHW060905280326
41934CB00007B/1189